HOW TO INTERPRET SCRIPTURE

Other Books by Frank M. Hasel

Adventists and Military Service:
Biblical, Historical, and Ethical Questions (2019)

Living for God (coming in 2020)

Longing for God: A Prayer and Bible Journal

Other Books by Michael G. Hasel

In the Footsteps of King David: Revelations From an Ancient
Biblical City (with Yosef Garfinkel and Saar Ganor)

Jerusalem: An Illustrated Archaeological Guide
(with Giselle S. Hasel)

The Promise: God's Everlasting Covenant
(with Gerhard F. Hasel)

Other Books by the Hasel family

A Thousand Shall Fall: The Electrifying Story of a Soldier and His
Family Who Dared to Practice Their Faith in Hitler's Germany
by Susi Hasel Mundy

HOW TO INTERPRET SCRIPTURE

FRANK M. HASEL AND MICHAEL G. HASEL

Pacific Press®
Publishing Association
Nampa, Idaho | www.pacificpress.com

Cover design resources from Lars Justinen

The authors assume full responsibility for the accuracy of all facts and quotations as cited in this book.

Unless otherwise indicated, Scripture quotations are from the New King James Version®. Copyright © 1982 by Thomas Nelson. Used by permission. All rights reserved.

Scripture quotations marked ESV are from The Holy Bible, English Standard Version® (ESV®), copyright © 2001 by Crossway, a publishing ministry of Good News Publishers. Used by permission. All rights reserved.

Scripture quotations marked KJV are from the King James Version of the Bible.

Scripture quotations marked NASB are from the NEW AMERICAN STANDARD BIBLE®, copyright © 1960, 1962, 1963, 1968, 1971, 1972, 1973, 1975, 1977, 1995 by the Lockman Foundation. Used by permission. www.lockman.org.

Scripture quotations marked NIV are from THE HOLY BIBLE, NEW INTERNATIONAL VERSION®. Copyright © 1973, 1978, 1984, 2011 by Biblica, Inc.® Used by permission. All rights reserved worldwide.

Scripture quotations marked RSV are from the Revised Standard Version of the Bible, copyright © 1946, 1952, 1971 by the Division of Christian Education of the National Council of the Churches of Christ in the U.S.A. Used by permission.

Additional copies of this book are available for purchase by calling toll-free 1-800-765-6955 or by visiting https://www.adventistbookcenter.com.

Library of Congress Cataloging-in-Publication Data

Names: Hasel, Frank M., 1962– author. | Hasel, Michael G., author.
Title: How to interpret scripture / Frank M. Hasel, Michael G. Hasel.
Description: Nampa, Idaho: Pacific Press Publishing Association, 2019. |
    Includes bibliographical references. | Summary: "How to Interpret Scripture reviews the subject
    of hermeneutics. It discusses a proper approach to Scripture and the use of principles of
    interpretation that will lead to sound conclusions"—Provided by publisher.
Identifiers: LCCN 2019034580 (print) | LCCN 2019034581 (ebook) | ISBN
    9780816365852 (paperback) | ISBN 9780816365869 (ebook)
Subjects: LCSH: Bible—Hermeneutics.
Classification: LCC BS476 .H3195 2019 (print) | LCC BS476 (ebook) | DDC
    220.601—dc23
LC record available at https://lccn.loc.gov/2019034580
LC e-book record available at https://lccn.loc.gov/2019034581

October 2019

Table of Contents

Introduction

As Seventh-day Adventist Christians, we believe in the importance of the Bible.[1] In fact, from the beginning, Adventist believers have considered themselves to be people of the Book, relying on it for guidance in matters of faith and practice. Through the years, the Bible has always been the foundation of our faith, and it ultimately determines what Seventh-day Adventists believe. Yet, in spite of its central place in our faith, biblical literacy seems to be waning. An increasing number of people no longer read and study the Bible. Moreover, strange teachings and even wild ideas are advanced by others, who solemnly claim these teachings and ideas derive from Scripture.

Thus, more is needed than the simple confession that the Bible is the foundation of our theology and the norm for our faith. This something more centers on the question of interpretation. How do we interpret the Bible adequately and correctly? How do we avoid the misuse and distortion of Scripture? How do we handle unstable people who twist the meaning of God's Word? Peter noted this challenge during his ministry, and the trend clearly continues today (2 Peter 3:16). Since Scripture tells us that people can misuse the Word of God and bend it to their own destruction, we must be on high alert and learn to interpret the Bible properly.

The stakes are high. If we approach the Bible with wrong presuppositions and poor methodologies, we will arrive at distorted conclusions. Our methods of interpretation have a direct bearing on our beliefs and practices. They affect our message and mission.

Our biblical interpretation also impacts our spirituality, affecting how we live and respond to the claims of Scripture. In a sense, the issue of biblical interpretation is like a theological watershed. An illustration of this is a drive on the famous German autobahn. Traveling southwest of Munich toward Lindau at Lake Constance, you cross into a lovely area of rolling hills in southern Bavaria. Not far from the city of Wangen (which happens to be the Hasels' city of origin), you will see a roadside sign that says "European Watershed." What it means is that the immediate area determines the flow of all the creeks and rivers in Central Europe. Here these tributaries are directed to one of two major rivers. The waters will flow into the river Danube and from there to the Black Sea, or they will flow into the Rhine, eventually spilling into the North Sea and the Atlantic Ocean. Fascinatingly, this area is not home to the towering Alps. Rather, it is full of gentle, rolling hills. But here the flow of the water is determined for Central Europe. No matter how many mountains stand in the way, the water flows persistently in two distinct directions: to the Black Sea in the east or to the North Sea.

In a similar fashion, the issue of our biblical interpretation shapes the outcome of our theology, message, and mission. It is common for modern biblical criticism to study the Bible just like any other book, not taking the divine dimension into consideration. Using this approach leads to vastly different conclusions than those that will be reached if we allow for the divine-human reality that Scripture affirms. If we seriously value what Scripture declares in many places—God speaks in and through the biblical writers—we have to allow that the method of our investigation of the Bible is determined by its object.[2] This means that we should not use methods that are alien to the divine dimension of Scripture. Instead, the principles of our Bible study must be consistent with the principles that govern our whole relationship with God. Thus, our study of Scripture should involve careful contemplation and devotional reflection, involving both the mind and the heart in the quest for true meaning. The divine reality of Scripture calls for a surrender of the interpreter to the authority of God's Written Word. Rather than criticizing the Word of God, we have to willingly stand under its authority and be transformed and judged by its message.

In this book, we want to outline the basic ideas that shape our understanding of the nature of Scripture. We will study how Jesus and the apostles viewed Scripture. We will reflect on the implications of what it means for the Bible to be the authoritative source of our theology. We will consider what it means when we say we follow the principle of *sola Scriptura*—"by Scripture alone." Naturally, the reading of Scripture involves interpretation, and correct methods of Bible study are indispensable to understand Scripture properly. We will illustrate the impact of different approaches by looking at the biblical story of Creation. We will also explore why history and prophecy are crucial for biblical faith. Finally, we will tackle the challenge of interpreting difficult passages of Scripture and simultaneously remaining faithful to the Word of God.

This book unfolds an approach to biblical interpretation that is in harmony with an important document officially affirmed by the Seventh-day Adventist Church: "Methods of Bible Study."[3] It is a resource for all who desire to study the Bible more diligently and to follow its teachings faithfully. It accompanies and provides additional information on the Seventh-day Adventist Church's second-quarter 2020 adult Bible study guide, *How to Interpret Scripture*.

Of course, this book can be read and studied independently, and we pray it will be a blessing to all who read it, leading them to a deeper understanding and greater love of the Word of God.

Not unto us, O LORD, not unto us,
But to Your name give glory,
Because of Your mercy,
Because of Your truth (Psalm 115:1).

---

1. The very first fundamental belief of the Seventh-day Adventist Church sets the stage for everything else we believe. It affirms, "The Holy Scriptures, Old and New Testaments, are the written Word of God, given by divine inspiration. The inspired authors spoke and wrote as they were moved by the Holy Spirit. In this Word, God has committed to humanity the knowledge necessary for salvation. The Holy Scriptures are the supreme, authoritative, and the infallible revelation of His will. They are the standard of character, the test of experience, the definitive revealer of doctrines, and the trustworthy record of God's acts in history." "Beliefs," Seventh-day Adventist Church, accessed June 6, 2019, https://www .adventist.org/en/beliefs/.

2. Time and again, biblical writers point away from themselves and to God as the Author of their message. Hence, this divine reality needs to be taken seriously when we want to come to grips with the Word of God. This has been aptly pointed out by Gerhard Maier in his book *Biblical Hermeneutics* (Wheaton, IL: Crossway Books, 1994), 20–26.

3. The statement "Methods of Bible Study" was approved and voted by the General Conference of Seventh-day Adventists Executive Committee at the Annual Council Session in Rio de Janeiro, Brazil, October 12, 1986, and can be found in *Statements, Guidelines, and Other Documents*, 4th ed. (Silver Spring, MD: General Conference of the Seventh-day Adventist Church, Communication Department, 2010), 241–250, or online at https://www.adventist.org/fileadmin /adventist.org/files/articles/official-statements/Statements-2010-english.pdf.

CHAPTER 1

The Uniqueness of the Bible

On August 21, 2017, the continental United States antici-pated a total solar eclipse. With painstaking scientific accuracy, astronomers had predicted the path of the eclipse. In order to maximize the experience, several important preparations were necessary:

1. Careful planning was required to be in the right place at the right time. While the path of the eclipse was predicted, special effort was required to travel to the path and position oneself in the total shadow.
2. Special safety glasses were needed to avoid damage to the retinas of the eyes. Staring at the sun causes permanent eye damage, and people were cautioned to view the eclipse with special glasses.

Hundreds of thousands of people drove across the country to experience the intensity of the eclipse's focal point, the umbra, as darkness covered the earth in a shadow of totality. Those who experienced it were awed by nature's predictability and overcome by the eeriness of the event.

Today, there is a deepening eclipse of God's Word. We have more access than ever to the Bible through print, apps, and translations in 3,350 languages.[1] Yet, in spite of this unprecedented access, enormous challenges remain.

Ignorance, superstition, and persecution

Looking back to the Dark Ages, we find that people did not own Bibles. The concept of righteousness by faith was not understood by the people, and the church leveraged this ignorance to influence the masses. For example, indulgences were introduced, promising that the purchased certificates offered reduced time in purgatory. In much of the world, that darkness continues to the present day. Significantly, one-third of the world's population will live and die without meeting a Christian or ever hearing the name of Jesus.[2] Billions live in countries where superstition and pagan religion keep them in fear and without hope. Wherever the Bible makes an impact and Christianity has attempted to enter, there has been massive persecution. Such was the case during the age of the Reformation, and it remains true today. In 2018, more than 215 million individuals around the globe were persecuted for their Christian faith.[3] In China, increasing numbers of churches are being closed, and pastors are imprisoned.

These facts demonstrate that much more work needs to be done in unreached places of the world before Jesus returns. Efforts need to be made to enter the dark areas that have eclipsed the Bible with error and to point people to the transforming power of God's Word.

Modernity, postmodernity, and relevance

After the Reformation, America provided a refuge for many persecuted Old World Christians. The separation of church and state was established, providing freedom of religion so that all could follow the dictates of their own conscience. The great Ivy League universities were established to train, based on the foundation of Scripture, a new generation of pastors, theologians, justices, and leaders. Harvard University students were obligated by Harvard's "Rules and Precepts" of 1646 to "exercise himselfe in reading the Scriptures twice a day that they bee ready to give an account of their proficiency therein . . . seeing the Entrance of the word giveth light."[4] More than fifty years later in 1701, as Harvard moved further away from its biblical foundations, Congregationalist Protestants established Yale University in Connecticut. The center of the university's seal contains a Bible with the words *Urim and Thummim*, surrounded by the Latin phrase *Lux et Veritas*, meaning "light and truth." Princeton University, which was established in 1746 in the wake of the First Great Awakening, has an official seal that contains the Bible with the words *Old and New Testament* in Latin and a motto that translates to "Under God's power, she flourishes." In his book *The Dying of the Light*, James Tunstead Burtchaell documents the gradual disengagement of higher education in America from its founding churches. The same disengagement can be documented in Protestant universities across the country.[5]

This separation was largely due to the acceptance of modern and postmodern philosophies that brought an element of criticism, elevating autonomous human reason above the Bible. In the twentieth century, the postmodernist agenda had all but erased any concept of absolute truth.[6] In the words of William F. Buckley Jr., "There is surely not a department at Yale that is uncontaminated with the absolute that there are no absolutes, no intrinsic rights, no ultimate truths."[7] The replacement of biblical presuppositions and assumptions with secular methods has resulted in the demise of most Christian institutions. Sadly, as education goes, so goes the church and society.

Distractions, apathy, and indifference

Contributing to the digression from biblical truth, the Barna Group has shown that 49 percent of "elders" and only 24 percent of millennials read their Bibles once a week.[8] At the same time, the market-research group Nielsen reports that the daily average screen time for adults in 2018 increased to eleven hours a day, up from nine hours and thirty-two minutes just four years earlier.[9] Attention spans have dropped at alarming rates as brains have been rewired, resulting in attention deficit hyperactivity disorder (ADHD) and attention deficit disorder (ADD) and increased depression.[10] Today, social media anxiety disorder has been recognized as an increasing problem as the overwhelming bombardment of media, day and night, decreases the desire to spend time with family and friends, not to mention studying the Bible.

Has technology and the media in our modern society brought us closer to happiness, peace, and harmonious living? School shootings have increased exponentially. In 2018 there were 97 school shootings in the United States alone—the highest in history.[11] Crime is multiplying. Everywhere we turn, in politics, economics, culture, education, job security, natural and global sustainability, energy resources, and food production, we are facing unprecedented challenges. Secular and religious thinkers alike recognize that our survival is at stake. Modernism has failed and so has its belief in progress and the arrival at ultimate truth through human reason and science alone.

Like the solar eclipse of 2017, the current eclipse of the Bible was predicted with unmistakable accuracy. Jesus foretold that there would come a time of great darkness when "they will deliver you up to tribulation and kill you, and you will be hated by all nations for My name's sake" (Matthew 24:9). Paul said, "For the time will come when they will not endure sound doctrine, but according to their own desires, because they have itching ears, they will heap up for themselves teachers; and they will turn their ears away from the truth, and be turned aside to fables" (2 Timothy 4:3, 4). John the revelator predicted that an end-time power will try to destroy God's Word: "The dragon was enraged with the woman [the church], and he went to make war with the rest of her offspring [the remnant], who keep the commandments of God and have the testimony of Jesus Christ" (Revelation 12:17).

How can we prepare for this intensifying time of confusion and darkness?

1. By taking our minds away from the distractions of

the world, looking to Jesus, and studying the signs of the times in God's Word.

2. Next, we "go" into the darkest places of the world "and make disciples of all the nations, baptizing them" and "teaching them to observe all things," as Jesus has commanded (Matthew 28:19, 20).

3. Finally, we must put on the glasses of protection as we gaze heavenward and keep our eyes fixed on the Son of Righteousness, so that we might have a proper interpretation of His Word. The glasses through which we view the world are our assumptions or presuppositions. When we approach Scripture we will want to interpret it according to the methods outlined by Christ and His apostles as revealed in the Bible, not the methods of modern and postmodern thinking. Jesus promises "Whoever believes in me, as Scripture has said, rivers of living water will flow from within them" (John 7:38).

How important is the study of the Bible? When Jesus was on earth, He highlighted His close connection to His Word. The *logos* or "word" came and "in Him was life, and the life was the light of men. And the light shines in the darkness" (John 1:4, 5). To rightly understand His mission and message, our first task is to understand the Scriptures correctly. They tell us all about Jesus, who is the Light of the world.

The power of the Bible

The Bible is the most unique and powerfully transforming book in human history. Composed of 66 books, written over 1,500 years on three continents, by over forty authors, the Bible is without equal in maintaining multiple threads of unity from Genesis to Revelation as it speaks on hundreds of different topics and issues.

Among the unique themes found only in the Bible are God's transcendence from Creation, His establishment of the seventh-day Sabbath, the holiness of God, the oneness of God in three (the Trinity), the righteousness of God, His personal *chesed*—love for all humanity, His redemption plan through the Messiah and His mediatorial work in the sanctuary, His eternal law as the basis of His government, His justice, and His work through the remnant of prophecy.[12] These, among other themes, are only taught within the linear view of the Bible from Creation to the Second Coming.

The Bible is unlike any other book in history when it comes to manuscript support. There are thousands of New Testament manuscripts preserved from the first four centuries after Christ.[13] For Plato, there are seven; Herodotus, only eight; and Homer's *Iliad* has merely 650 surviving copies.[14] No other ancient literature comes close in terms of the number of copies and shortness of time between the originals and the copies.

The Dead Sea Scrolls, discovered by accident in 1947, testify to the Old Testament's accuracy over millennia. Copyists carefully worked in the desert to meticulously reproduce the manuscripts, which predated by more than one thousand years the medieval manuscripts our translations were based on. We can read the entire book of Isaiah and see the remarkable way in which God preserved its accuracy over centuries of scribal work so that today we can rely on the Bibles we hold in our hands.[15]

The Bible was the first massive book ever translated by a group of Jewish scribes in Alexandria. Printed by Johannes Gutenberg in A.D. 1454–1455, it was the first mass-produced book published on a movable-type printing press. It has been widely distributed in many languages and maintains its place as a perennial bestseller. Today, it can be read by the vast majority of the earth's population.

Furthermore, the Bible has survived major attempts to eliminate or nullify its contents, whether during the Christian persecution by the Roman emperor Diocletian, the French Revolution, or today's postmodern secularism. Not only has it survived, but it has also flourished, inspiring the greatest works of music, art, and literature ever created.

The Bible is also unique in its content and message. It focuses on the plan of salvation and God's redemptive acts in history. Unlike other religious books, it is constituted in history and, therefore, can be confirmed through archaeological and historical research. The Bible and history are intertwined in the prophetic foretelling of God's future plans and His eternal kingdom. The Bible speaks equally to men and women and to people of different social, economic, and educational levels. It inspires, ennobles, and effects enormous change. It is the *living* Word of God because the same Spirit of God through which Scripture was inspired (2 Timothy 3:16, 17) is promised to believers today to guide us into all truth as we study the Word (John 14:17; 15:26; 16:13).

A precious gift

The Bible, a priceless gift and legacy, cannot be taken for granted because it was purchased with a weighty price. Recently, I had the privilege of holding a rare Bible. Only two complete copies have survived. One is in a library in Nice, France, and the other rested in my white-gloved hands. It was the New Testament translated into French by Jacques Lefèvre d'Étaples during the Reformation, around A.D. 1524. This was the first Bible ever printed in French and the first printed New Testament to have made its way to the Waldensian valleys. (Some of the Waldenses were known as the *insabbatati* or *sabbatati* because they kept the seventh-day Sabbath.[16])

> Their mission was to reform the Church and to call Christians back to faithfulness to the Bible, in spite of bloody persecutions and massacres that nearly exterminated them. They traveled extensively through Europe and were sowing the seeds that contributed to the coming Protestant Reformation. Their work influenced Wycliffe and his followers and Hus and Jerome and their followers, and their influence came to full fruition in the time of the Anabaptists, Luther, Zwingli, and Calvin. They have given Protestants an inspiring example of faithfulness to the Word of God in times of great apostasy and ruthless persecution.[17]

What makes this Book so precious is not its scarcity but the reason behind it.

The Waldenses were declared heretics and hunted to near extinction.[18] Their Bibles were collected and burned. Before Luther translated the Bible into German for the people, this New Testament had existed for the French-speaking faithful in the valleys of northern Italy and Switzerland and spread from there to the rest of Europe. Young Waldensian students carried excerpts of the Bible with them to the universities in the lowlands to witness of the power of the Word.[19] Today, their resolve remains a testament of faithfulness and determination in the midst of the severest of trials.

Scripture's destination and hope

It is the journey that matters, not the destination: this has become the mantra of our postmodern culture today. The sad reality is that our focus has shifted to the journey because many no longer know where they are going. They have lost all sense of direction and the pursuit of any destination. Could it be that in humanity's desire to free itself from all absolutes, it has become empty, lost, and without hope?

Here we must reintroduce the Bible. The God who inspired it provides for the deepest longings of the human heart, giving it purpose and direction. Happiness does not revolve around an existential journey that focuses on oneself; rather, happiness revolves around the saving grace of Jesus Christ. God, through His active work in history and through the divine word of prophecy, gives each person purpose, hope, and a future. This is why Moses, as he approached his own death on Mount Nebo, could offer these words: "Set your hearts on all the words which I testify among you today, which you shall command your children to be careful to observe—all the words of this law. For it is not a futile thing for you, *because it is your life*, and *by this word* you shall prolong your days in the land which you cross over the Jordan to possess" (Deuteronomy 32:46, 47; emphasis added).

It is the understanding of God's Word that brings life. It contains directions to the Promised Land, given by Jesus

Himself. He promised to "prepare a place for [us]" and affirmed, "I am the way, the truth, and the life. No one comes to the Father except through Me" (John 14:2, 6). According to Jesus, it is the journey that matters because it is all about the destination.

Our task in this book is to examine the role of Scripture and learn how to rightly study its holy pages. This quest will reward us with an understanding of God's covenant plan of redemption for a lost planet. When we understand His message, we will understand the joy, hope, and peace that make His revelation more relevant today than at any other time in earth's history.

---

1. Statistics for 2018 include the complete Bible in 683 languages, the New Testament in 1,534 languages, and parts of the Bible in 1,133 languages for a total of 3,350 languages with some Scripture. See "Scripture and Language Statistics 2018," Wycliffe Global Alliance, accessed April 30, 2019, http://www.wycliffe .net/statistics.

2. Paul Strand, " 'More Than One-Third of Humanity Will Never Hear About Jesus': Day to Reach the Unreached Set for May 20," CBN, April 28, 2018, https:// www1.cbn.com/cbnnews/cwn/2018/april/more-than-one-third-of-humanity-will -never-hear-about-jesus-day-to-reach-the-unreached-set-for-may-20.

3. Lindy Lowry, "215 Million Believers Face Persecution for Their Faith in Christ," Open Doors, January 10, 2018, https://www.opendoorsusa.org/christian -persecution/stories/215-million-believers-persecution-for-their-faith-in-christ/.

4. Samuel Eliot Morison, *The Founding of Harvard College* (Cambridge, MA: Harvard University Press, 1963), 333.

5. James Tunstead Burtchaell, *The Dying of the Light: The Disengagement of Colleges and Universities From Their Christian Churches* (Grand Rapids, MI: Eerdmans, 1998); cf. George M. Marsden, *The Soul of the American University: From Protestant Establishment to Established Unbelief* (New York: Oxford University Press, 1994).

6. See the insightful critique of this trend in higher education by Allan Bloom, *The Closing of the American Mind* (New York: Simon and Schuster, 1987).

7. William F. Buckley Jr., *God and Man at Yale*, 50th anniversary ed. (Washington, DC: Regnery, 1986), 23.

8. "The Bible in America: 6-Year Trends," Barna, June 15, 2016, https://www .barna.com /research/the-bible-in-america-6-year-trends/.

9. Quentin Fottrell, "People Spend Most of Their Waking Hours Staring at Screens," *MarketWatch*, August 4, 2018, https://www.marketwatch.com/story /people-are-spending-most-of-their-waking-hours-staring-at-screens-2018-08-01.

10. On media in general, see Richard Restak, *The New Brain: How the Modern Age Is Rewiring Your Mind* (New York: Rodale, 2003); more recently on social media, see Melissa G. Hunt et al., "No More FOMO: Limiting Social Media Decreases Loneliness and Depression," *Journal of Social and Clinical Psychology* 37,

no. 10 (November 2018): 751–768; Liu yi Lin et al., "Association Between Social Media Use and Depression Among U.S. Young Adults," *Depression and Anxiety* 33, no. 4 (January 2016): 323–331.

11. "The School Shootings of 2018: What's Behind the Numbers," *Education Week*, December 19, 2018, https://www.edweek.org/ew/section/multimedia/the -school-shootings-of-2018-whats-behind.html.

12. Norman H. Snaith, *The Distinctive Ideas of the Old Testament* (New York: Schocken, 1964); see articles in Raoul Dederen, ed., *Handbook of Seventh-day Adventist Theology* (Hagerstown, MD: Review and Herald®, 2000).

13. On New Testament manuscript support, see Bruce M. Metzger, *The Text of the New Testament: Its Transmission, Corruption, and Restoration*, 3rd ed. (New York: Oxford University Press, 1992), 33–35.

14. Lee Strobel, *The Case for Christ* (Grand Rapids, MI: Zondervan, 1998), 75–82.

15. Gleason L. Archer, *A Survey of Old Testament Introduction*, rev. ed. (Chicago: Moody, 1994), 29.

16. P. Gerard Damsteegt, "Decoding Ancient Waldensian Names: New Discoveries," *Andrews University Seminary Studies* 54, no. 2 (Autumn 2016): 237–258.

17. P. Gerard Damsteegt, "The Ancient Waldenses: Did the Reformation Predate Luther?" *Ministry*, October 2017, 24, 25.

18. Gabriel Audisio, *The Waldensian Dissent: Persecution and Survival, c. 1170– c. 1570* (New York: Cambridge University Press, 1999), 15–17; Earle E. Cairns, *Christianity Through the Centuries: A History of the Christian Church*, 3rd ed. (Grand Rapids, MI: Zondervan, 1996), 221; Peter Biller, *The Waldenses, 1170– 1530: Between a Religious Order and a Church* (Burlington, VT: Ashgate, 2002), 191; King Alfonso II of Aragon, "Edictum contra haereticos," quoted in Giovanni Gonnet, *Enchiridion fontium Valdensium: Recueil critique de sources concernant les Vaudois au moyen âge du IIIe concile de Latran au Synode de Chanforan, 1179–1532* (Torre Pellice, Italy: Claudiana, 1958), 92.

19. Ellen G. White, *The Great Controversy* (Nampa, ID: Pacific Press®, 2002), 69, 70.

CHAPTER 2

The Origin and Nature
of the Bible

For centuries, the Bible has played an authoritative role in Christian theology. It has been aptly said that "the Christian community that abandons the authority of the biblical witness becomes little more than the mouthpiece of whatever current cultural norms catch its fancy."[1] The authoritative role of Scripture, however, is significantly determined by our understanding of the origin of the Written Word of God. Our knowledge of the origin of Scripture, in turn, is shaped by our understanding of the nature of what we call the process of revelation and inspiration.

Throughout history, there have been various interpretations of the nature and function of inspiration. These differing concepts of inspiration have substantially impacted our understanding of the nature of the Bible, its trustworthiness, its reliability, its ultimate authority, and the interpretational principles used to comprehend it. Unfortunately, the lack of a clear-cut and unified terminology has complicated the entire discussion, making it a challenge to have a meaningful conversation about the subject. Nevertheless, there are a few basic concepts surrounding inspiration and the authority of Scripture that need to be understood, even within the Seventh-day Adventist Church.

No supernatural inspiration

Current concepts of inspiration include an approach that developed in the wake of the Enlightenment. In this school of thought, classical liberal theology denies any supernatural inspiration. The origination of Scripture is not from above but from below—that is, from within the closed flow of human history. Since a purely naturalistic understanding of the world leaves no room for supernatural involvement, divine inspiration is disallowed. Consequently, "inspiration" in this view is a purely natural and human phenomenon, perhaps comparable to the inspired genius of Shakespeare, Luther, or Mozart.

From this perspective, Scripture has to be studied and interpreted like any other book; it is approached as if God does not exist. And without divine inspiration, the Bible only reflects the historical and cultural circumstances that produced it. The absence of divine inspiration defaults the study of God's Word to the cultural and socioeconomic influences that shaped the biblical text.

This approach—a belief that the Bible is strictly a product of its times—naturally divests the Scriptures of divine authority. In this understanding of Scripture, one only needs to appeal to the intrinsic factors and the principle of analogy, using current knowledge to interpret events in the distant past.

Furthermore, in this school of thought, the Bible has to be studied historicocritically, which means there is a methodological criticism where Scripture cannot be trusted. Such critical scholarship never leads to any certainty of belief but makes every individual event uncertain.[2] It produces only probabilities that raise questions about the certainty of faith.[3] Christianity and the Bible lose their uniqueness, for they can only be understood in relation to the whole of history.[4] As a purely human book, the Bible is characterized by theological diversity, contradictions, and errors. There is no theological unity in Scripture, only a plurality of conflicting and even mutually exclusive voices that reflect the diversity of its original setting and the biblical writers. In this scenario, Scripture is just like any other book; it is full of mistakes and even deficient ethical

22

viewpoints. Here, human reason rather than Scripture is the ultimate norm for what should and should not be accepted.

Verbal inspiration

At the other end of the interpretational spectrum is an approach called verbal inspiration. It embraces God as one who is capable of using human language to communicate His will to human beings. Scripture originates from God above rather than from men below. This understanding of inspiration appeals to statements like the one found in 2 Timothy 3:16, where the apostle Paul states that *Scripture* is "God-breathed" or God inspired (NIV). In this view, the locus of inspiration is predominantly on the inspired product, on the written words of Scripture, rather than on the minds of the biblical writers. Since there is an emphasis on the words, the *verbum* of Scripture, the name for this view is verbal inspiration.

This understanding of inspiration, while taking seriously some statements of Scripture, is often influenced by a strong Calvinistic view of divine predestination, leading proponents to believe that God in His sovereignty predetermined the very words used in producing the Bible. Thus, the words of Scripture share in His divine perfection, becoming infallible and inerrant in every detail. Such an understanding of inspiration is often associated, especially by its liberal critics, with a strict, mechanical view of inspiration that borders on divine dictation; the idea that God directly conveyed the words used by the Bible writers.

During the time of the Protestant Orthodoxy, a few representatives of verbal inspiration even claimed that God dictated the very letters and even the vowel points of the Hebrew text of the Old Testament, effectively eliminating any genuine human involvement in the origin of Scripture. While few modern representatives of verbal inspiration uphold such a rigid understanding, the words of Scripture are still associated with the concepts of inerrancy and perfection. The resulting image is of Scripture being written by God's hand with the biblical writers functioning as His pen. Such an approach can lead to the neglect of historical context and a subsequent misinterpretation of many Bible passages.

Representatives of this understanding of Scripture view it as having divine authority and sharing divine perfection. Because of its divine inspiration, they affirm its theological unity and teach biblical truth with a high level of certainty. Rather than acknowledging internal contradictions and errors within the Bible, verbal inspirationists are eager to harmonize its statements. They believe the internal unity of Scripture is the work of the Holy Spirit in the process of inspiration, and because the Holy Spirit is at work, the Bible cannot and should not be studied like just any other book; the divine component needs to be taken seriously. History is also studied but plays a minor interpretational role. Inspiration, then, is God at work through the individual biblical author in such a way that the very words employed are perfectly capable of transmitting divine truth and conveying God's message without errors and mistakes.

Thought inspiration

In another approach, some Bible students have shifted the focus away from specific wording. In this view, the primary place of inspiration is in the thoughts of the biblical writers and not in the words they employ. In a sense, this position is a reaction to the mechanical verbal-inspiration view that seeks to elevate the divine factor. Thought inspiration upholds the idea of supernatural inspiration from above but leaves the process of recording the results of that inspiration entirely to the prophet; the biblical writers freely choose their own words.

While it is true that Bible writers enjoy genuine freedom, representatives of thought inspiration often associate another problematic idea. This idea involves the belief that everything human is automatically fallible and prone to error. Hence, the language used to convey inspired thoughts is, at best, imperfect, lending itself to discrepancies and mistakes. This presupposition places the judgment of what is trustworthy and what is fallible squarely in the hands of the interpreter, making him the final arbiter of truth rather than the Holy Scriptures. While it is true that God granted Bible writers great freedom to express themselves in their unique style, their humanity does not automatically render the Bible fallible. Even in their sinfulness, human beings are fully capable of communicating truth. Should not God be able to communicate effectively with the creatures He has created? After all, He is the Author of language, and truthfulness is one of His character traits (Exodus 20:16). Furthermore, thoughts are only known to us through human words! Without expressing our thoughts in adequate words, we would not know any of God's inspired thoughts.

Thus, while inspiration works at the thought level, there must also be some effect on the product that expresses those thoughts. Otherwise the concept of inspiration is utterly useless. By discounting the authority of the written page, the thought-inspiration approach to biblical interpretation falls short of "rightly dividing the word of truth" (2 Timothy 2:15). This deficiency has led Bible students to propose yet another concept of inspiration that resolves the issue.

Plenary or entire inspiration

Instead of focusing on predetermined words by eliminating genuine human freedom or by restricting the process of inspiration to thought inspiration, careful students of Scripture have affirmed what is called plenary inspiration. According to *Merriam-Webster*, the word *plenary* denotes "complete in every aspect" or "fully attended or constituted by all entitled to be present."[5] Thus, rather than eliminating the freedom of the human component or denying divine supervision in the process of inspiration, a plenary view of inspiration keeps both biblically attested factors in balance. One recent biblical scholar has called it "entire inspiration."[6] This wording and concept are derived directly from the Bible and are rooted in 2 Timothy 3:16, where we read that "*all* Scripture is given by inspiration of God" (emphasis added). By "all Scripture," Paul means either the whole of the Scripture of his day or "every passage of Scripture," including various parts of the Bible.[7]

Plenary or entire inspiration avoids the imbalances of verbal and thought inspiration. Adventist authors on the subject have stated: "Whether inspiration should be attributed to the inspired writers or to the Scriptures written by them is to a large extent a needless dilemma."[8] Indeed, the Bible states that the Holy Spirit moved upon the biblical writers (2 Peter 1:19, 21; 1 Thessalonians 2:13). It is clear that the first locus of inspiration is on the thoughts of the biblical writers. However, it follows that what they produced was inspired and became the inspired Word of God. Adventists recognize that "there is little doubt that thoughts as well as words are involved in this process."[9] Inspired persons received visions, dreams, and impressions from God in visual or verbal form, and these they conveyed faithfully and truthfully as they had received them.

While the words written by them are distinctly human, biblical writers emphasize that their words are nevertheless the Word of God. A plenary understanding of Scripture preserves the divine character of the Bible while also giving the historical context its due consideration.

In verbal, thought, or plenary (entire) inspiration, the process of inspiration functions on the individual or verbal level. More recently, another concept of inspiration has also been proposed.

Inspiration of the community

Paul Achtemeier suggests that the process of inspiration does not function so much on the individual level but on the community level. The proclamation of the community of faith and its witness to the living Lord is elevated to the point where it becomes "the Word of God in all its timely relevance for the historic juncture at which we live."[10] Rather than working on chosen individuals to communicate His will, God grants inspiration to the entire faith community.

By this, Achtemeier means that the Bible can no longer be regarded as the Word of God.[11] In fact, for Achtemeier, the only equation with the Word of God that is found in the New Testament is the person of Jesus of Nazareth. Thus, the Bible contains the Word of God (Jesus) in the many human words of its writers, echoing the famous distinction of Karl Barth, for whom the Bible is but a witness to the testified Word of God,

Jesus.[12] The Bible is no longer the normative Written Word of God; it only contains the witness to the Word of God and may become the Word of God in preaching.

However, in the Bible, we find no indication that the entire community is inspired, as Achtemeier seems to believe. To elevate the proclamation of the community of faith to the level where it becomes the Word of God does not adequately account for distortions in its proclamation and the witness of the church. Without divinely inspired Scripture as a guiding norm, the proclamation of the church and its teachings become a "nose of wax" whose actual shape can be twisted in whatever way one wants to go, depending on one's theological creativity. Here Scripture has at best a functional authority[13] in the life of the church but lacks its unity and divinely inspired authority.

The divine-human character of Scripture

Taking the divine-human character of Scripture seriously avoids the pitfall of viewing the Bible as a purely human product over which people stand as judges. It motivates us to treat biblical words with respect and love. It encourages humble and honest inquiry, allowing the Bible to shape our lives and worldviews.

Our love for God's Word will create a desire to follow it faithfully. Recognizing the Bible as the inspired Word of God fosters deep faith in Him, trust in His Word, and confidence that the Bible is a reliable guide for practical Christian living. We respect the words of Scripture because they communicate the truth about God as revealed to the minds of the biblical writers. This understanding leads to an interpretation of Scripture that values everything written on a particular subject and allows Scripture to be its own interpreter.

---

1. Paul J. Achtemeier, *Inspiration and Authority: Nature and Function of Christian Scripture* (Peabody, MA: Hendrickson, 1999), 148.

2. Edgar Krenz, *The Historical-Critical Method* (Philadelphia: Fortress Press, 1989), 55.

3. Krenz, *The Historical-Critical Method*, 57.

4. Krenz, 56.

5. *Merriam-Webster.com Dictionary*, s.v. "plenary," accessed April 30, 2019,

https://www.merriam-webster.com/dictionary/plenary.

6. Gerhard Maier, *Biblical Hermeneutics* (Wheaton, IL: Crossway Books, 1994), 120–124.

7. Cf. Gerhard F. Hasel, *Understanding the Living Word of God* (Mountain View, CA: Pacific Press®, 1980), 69.

8. Peter M. van Bemmelen, "Revelation and Inspiration," in *Handbook of Seventh-day Adventist Theology*, ed. Raoul Dederen (Hagerstown, MD: Review and Herald®, 2000), 39. On Ellen G. White's similarly balanced view of the process of revelation and inspiration, see Frank M. Hasel, "Revelation and Inspiration," in *The Ellen G. White Encyclopedia*, ed. Denis Fortin and Jerry Moon (Hagerstown, MD: Review and Herald®, 2014), 1087–1101.

9. Van Bemmelen, "Revelation and Inspiration," 40.

10. Achtemeier, *Inspiration and Authority*, 159.

11. Achtemeier, 158.

12. Cf. Karl Barth, *Church Dogmatics: The Doctrine of God*, vol. 2, pt. 2 (London: T & T Clark, 2004), 457ff. See also Frank M. Hasel, "The Christological Analogy of Scripture in Karl Barth," *Theologische Zeitschrift* 50, no. 1 (1994): 41–49.

13. Achtemeier, *Inspiration and Authority*, 146.

3

Jesus' and the Apostles' View of the Bible

The cry of the Reformation was *ad fontes*, meaning "back to the sources." This means that the Reformers decided to go back to the source of Scripture to truly understand the nature of Christianity, rather than rely on the traditions of the medieval church. This crucial pivot to the original sources brought a renewed focus on the Scriptures, transforming the way people looked at the world.

The question of authority

Yet today, the traditions and methods of medieval scholastic philosophy utilized before the Reformation continue to be employed. Scripture is often understood only through the lens of philosophy or nature. Enlightenment philosophy brought into question basic biblical inspiration and authority, relegating the words of God to the words of men, which were written in a particular time and setting. As theologian Krister Stendahl, the former dean of Harvard University's Divinity School, writes, these new assumptions mean that the modern interpreter must distinguish between "what it [a Bible passage] meant and what it means." In other words, there is a "tension between the mind of a Semitic past and the thought of modern man."[1]

For example, what a passage may have meant to an ancient

rabbinic scholar like Paul addressing a local situation in Ephesus or Corinth, may not be at all what the Bible means today. It cannot mean the same thing because, according to this view, the modern world's scientific knowledge and understanding were completely unknown to the ancients. The biblical writers were said to be reflecting a local cultural situation, and we modern readers need to interpret the Bible by today's standards. Biblical faith seems largely irrelevant in an age of electricity, computers, and smartphone technology.

Lutheran theologian Rudolf Bultmann attempted to rescue Christianity from the effects of modern historicocritical thinking by engaging in an exercise of "demythologizing" the New Testament. He reinterpreted miracles and other supernatural concepts such as the resurrection and divine nature of Christ to make it acceptable to the modern mind. For Bultmann, "mythological conceptions of heaven and hell are no longer acceptable for modern men, since for scientific thinking to speak of 'above' and 'below' in the universe has lost all meaning."[2] For Bultmann, "it is mere wishful thinking to suppose that the ancient world-view of the Bible can be renewed."[3]

But this accommodation to the presuppositions of materialism and modernism also raises important questions about the nature of the Bible and the teachings of Jesus and the apostles. In the minds of Jesus and the apostles, was there a difference between what the Bible meant and what it means? Did Jesus and the apostles accept the reality of miracles in the Old Testament and teach that miracles still occurred in their day? How did they relate to the people, places, and events described? What were their assumptions and subsequent methods of interpretation? As Jesus and His disciples met the skeptical and cynical teachers of the law, how did they respond to their questions? Like the Reformers, we need to return to the sources to understand how the biblical writers and Jesus interpreted the Bible.

Jesus' view of Scripture
Jesus affirms the authority of Scripture in various ways. First, He accepts the miracles in the Old Testament as authentic. In

Matthew 12:40, He says, "For as Jonah was three days and three nights in the belly of the great fish, so will the Son of Man be three days and three nights in the heart of the earth." Jesus not only confirms Jonah's experience in the belly of the fish, but He also predicts His own experience after the Crucifixion, foreshadowing His three days in the tomb. He goes on to say, "The men of Nineveh will rise up in the judgment with this generation and condemn it, because they repented at the preaching of Jonah; and indeed a greater than Jonah is here" (verse 41). He views the events surrounding Jonah's preaching to the Ninevites as historical and trustworthy.

In another example, Jesus says, "All too well you reject the commandment of God, that you may keep your tradition. For Moses said, 'Honor your father and your mother'; and, 'He who curses father or mother, let him be put to death' " (Mark 7:9, 10). He not only confirms the commandments of God by referring to the fifth commandment, but He also points out that they were given to the people by Moses. Likewise, Jesus affirms Moses' teachings by instructing the healed leper to "go and show yourself to the priest, and make an offering for your cleansing, as a testimony to them, just as Moses commanded" (Luke 5:14). The record shows that Jesus accepts the historical reality of many Bible characters; among them are Abel (Matthew 23:35), David (Matthew 12:3), and Zechariah (Matthew 23:35), among others.

Jesus also keeps the commandments and urges others to do likewise: "If you love Me, keep My commandments" (John 14:15). He offers pointed counsel to the rich young ruler: "But if you want to enter into life, keep the commandments." The young man responds by asking which ones. Jesus replies, " 'You shall not murder,' 'You shall not commit adultery,' 'You shall not steal,' 'You shall not bear false witness,' 'Honor your father and your mother,' and, 'You shall love your neighbor as yourself' " (Matthew 19:17–19). In addition to this affirmation of the commandments found in Exodus, Jesus is also careful to keep the seventh-day Sabbath (Luke 4), bringing focus to its original purpose. "The Sabbath was made for man, not man for the Sabbath" (Mark 2:27, NIV), and "the Son of Man is also Lord of the Sabbath" (Luke 6:5).

In the Sermon on the Mount, Jesus highlights the enduring nature of the law: "Do not think that I came to destroy the Law or the Prophets. I did not come to destroy but to fulfill. . . . One jot or one tittle will by no means pass from the law till all is fulfilled" (Matthew 5:17, 18). This "faith comes by hearing, and hearing by the word of God" (Romans 10:17). To the Sadducees, He says, "You are wrong, because you know neither the Scriptures nor the power of God" (Matthew 22:29, RSV). These passages show that Jesus viewed Scripture as foundational to our lives and experience.

Jesus' use of Scripture

Christ's life displayed the Scriptures' authoritative place in His experience and ministry. Christ was baptized by John the Baptist, and the visible manifestation of the Holy Spirit in the form of a dove ratified His ministry. At the same time, the Father pronounced His blessing, "This is My beloved Son, in whom I am well pleased" (Matthew 3:17). The Spirit immediately led Jesus into the Judean wilderness where, in a weakened condition, He was tempted by Satan. This epic encounter was a decisive moment in Christ's ministry. Would He stand the test?

The first encounter centered on appetite and appealed to the human penchant for self-preservation. Jesus responded by quoting Deuteronomy: "It is written, 'Man shall not live by bread alone, but by every word that proceeds from the mouth of God' " (Matthew 4:4). His defense was a retreat to the living Word and its divine source, thereby affirming the authority of Scripture. Next, Satan tempted Jesus with the love of display and presumption. Jesus responded, "It is written again, 'You shall not tempt the LORD your God' " (verse 7; cf. Luke 4:12). Finally, Jesus was tempted to succumb to pride and to grasp dominion of the world's kingdoms. His response was quick and sure: "It is written, 'You shall worship the LORD your God, and Him only you shall serve' " (Luke 4:8). In the end, true worship for Jesus was focused on God. Submission to His Word was true worship.

In all three temptations, Jesus responds with the words "It is written." Notice, He does not say, "It was written" or "It will be written." Instead, He uses the present tense: "It *is* written." He does so because the Word of God is not relegated to a past culture nor is it meant only for future generations. No, it is the living Word of God that applies to all people and all nations for all time. The Word was present truth for Moses and Christ and still is for us today.

The wilderness encounter is proof that Jesus' method of defense against the attacks of the adversary was singular; it was the Bible and the Bible only. Though He was God, His defense was a complete submission to the Word of God. He did not lean on opinion, convoluted arguments, or barbed animosity. He boldly quoted Scripture. For Christ, Scripture had the greatest authority—the greatest power. In this way, His ministry began with a secure foundation, built on the trustworthiness of the Bible.

At Calvary, Jesus' final words also testify to the authority of Scripture. In two utterances from the cross, He quotes prophetic words from the Old Testament. In the first case, "Jesus cried out with a loud voice, saying, 'Eli, Eli, lama sabachthani?' that is, 'My God, My God, why have You forsaken Me?' " (Matthew 27:46). Here, He is quoting Psalm 22:1. A few verses later, this same chapter says,

I am poured out like water,
And all My bones are out of joint;
My heart is like wax. . . .
You have brought Me to the dust of death. . . .
They pierced My hands and My feet;
I can count all My bones.
They look and stare at Me.
They divide My garments among them,
And for My clothing they cast lots (verses 14–18).

In the second case, Jesus quotes again from the same psalm: "It is finished!" (John 19:30). Walter Kaiser Jr. writes, "It is no coincidence. . . . It indicates that on the cross the mind of our Lord was instructed, comforted, and encouraged by the contents of this psalm."[4] But there is more; Jesus is pointing the witnesses of every era to clear Old Testament prophecies concerning the nature of His death, thereby affirming the authority and accuracy of Scripture in predicting His suffering. Charles Briggs writes, "These sufferings [in Psalm 22] transcend those of any historical sufferer, with the single exception of Jesus Christ. They find their exact counterpart in the sufferings of the cross."[5]

At the foot of the cross, the disciples hardly understood these statements. They were confused and despondent. How could this have happened? Jesus' humiliating death was not the deliverance they expected from their Messiah. But in the following days, their spirits were buoyed by conversations with Jesus. In these post-crucifixion encounters, Jesus again affirmed the method by which they should have studied Scripture.

Luke 24 records two of these appearances. First, Jesus joins two believers on the road to Emmaus and explains how He was the fulfillment of the Old Testament Messianic prophecies. "And beginning with Moses and all the Prophets, he interpreted to them in all the Scriptures the things concerning himself" (Luke 24:27, ESV).

After their stunning Emmaus-road experience, the two disciples raced to share the good news with the other disciples. As they told their story, Jesus appeared to the entire group and reminded them that His life was the fulfillment of Scripture: "These are my words . . . that everything written about me in the Law of Moses and the Prophets and the Psalms must be fulfilled." He then "opened their minds to understand the Scriptures" (verses 44, 45, ESV).

In the first instance, on the road to Emmaus, note the specific reference "*all the Scriptures*" (verse 27, ESV; emphasis added). The appeal to Scripture is later reemphasized in the second passage to the disciples as the "Law of Moses, the Prophets and the Psalms" (verse 44, ESV). The mention of the Law of Moses, the prophets, and the psalms refers to the three divisions of the Bible as understood by the Jews of His day. The Torah is the law, or the instruction, and is composed of the first five books of the Bible. The *Nevi'im* are the prophets, and the *Ketuvim*, which included the book of Psalms, are the writings.

These exchanges establish that Jesus, the Word made flesh (John 1:1–3), relied on the authority of Scripture to explain how His life and ministry were foretold hundreds of years earlier. By referring to the totality of Scripture, Jesus was teaching the disciples by example. As they went forth to spread the gospel message, they too were to expound all Scripture, bringing power and understanding to new converts. They were to allow Scripture to interpret Scripture, a methodology that the Protestants would later refer to as *Sola Scriptura*.

In Matthew 28:18–20, Jesus gave the gospel commission to His disciples, "All authority in heaven and on earth has been given to me" (ESV). This authority was rooted in His Father and the entire Godhead. "Go therefore and make disciples of all nations, baptizing them in the name of the Father and of the Son and of the Holy Spirit" (ESV). Following this stirring charge, He leaves them one final directive: they were to teach all nations "to observe all that I have commanded you" (ESV). And what did Jesus teach and command? He taught *all* of Scripture. It was upon the prophetic authority of the Word that He came, and it was in fulfillment of the prophecies of Scripture that He submitted to His Father. Ellen G. White writes, "[Christ] pointed to the Scriptures as of unquestionable authority, and we should do the same. The Bible is to be presented as the word of the infinite God, as the end of all controversy and the foundation of all faith."[6]

Apostles' view of Scripture

As one would expect, the apostles also accepted the historicity and accuracy of the Old Testament. Of the Exodus experience, Luke wrote, "He brought them out, after he had shown wonders and signs in the land of Egypt, and in the Red Sea, and in the wilderness forty years" (Acts 7:36). Paul writes in Hebrews, "By faith they passed through the Red Sea as by dry land, whereas the Egyptians, attempting to do so, were drowned" (Hebrews 11:29). Speaking of the Exodus, Princeton University scholar Otto Piper calculated that of the 2,688 uses of the Old Testament in the New Testament, "Exodus occupies the third place with c. 220 quotations."[7] These frequent references mean that the events, themes, and theology of the Exodus served as a basis for the thinking and perspective of Jesus and the New Testament writers.[8] The Exodus and the journey into the Promised Land served as a type of God's miraculous deliverance from the bondage of sin and our journey to the heavenly home Jesus is preparing for us. But this was not limited to the Exodus; the entire New Testament consistently refers to the Old Testament as an authoritative source.

In Romans 1:2, Paul refers to the Old Testament as "the holy scriptures" (RSV), and in Romans 3:2, he refers to it as the "oracles of God" (RSV) or the "words of God" (NIV). Peter said with great emphasis, "No prophecy of Scripture is of any private interpretation, for prophecy never came by the will of man, but holy men of God spoke as they were moved by the Holy Spirit" (2 Peter 1:20, 21). In the same way, the Scriptures elevate the New Testament to this level. Jesus said to His disciples, "He who hears you hears Me" (Luke 10:16).

Numerous New Testament books claim inspiration. Peter refers to the writings of Paul as part of "the rest of the Scriptures" (2 Peter 3:16). Paul claims the Holy Spirit as the source of his epistles (1 Corinthians 7:40; 14:37; 2 Corinthians 3:5, 6; 4:13). John introduces the Apocalypse as "the Revelation of Jesus Christ, which God gave Him to show His servants—things which must shortly take place" (Revelation 1:1). At the end of the book, we are told,

> "These words are faithful and true. . . .
> ". . . Blessed is he who keeps the words of the prophecy of this book" (Revelation 22:6, 7).

Jesus' and the Apostles' View of the Bible

In summary, based on the claims of Jesus and the apostles, the Bible cannot be interpreted in the same manner as other human books. "The only true, adequate, and appropriate hermeneutic of the Bible as the Word of God in human form must be a hermeneutic *of* Scripture, a hermeneutic *by* Scripture, and a hermeneutic *for* Scripture, in short, a biblical hermeneutic."[9] Ellen G. White also understood the unique nature of the Word of God, reminding her readers that "the Bible is its own expositor."[10]

---

1. Krister Stendahl, "Biblical Theology, Contemporary," in *The Interpreter's Dictionary of the Bible*, vol. 1, ed. George A. Buttrick (New York: Abingdon, 1962), 419, 420.

2. Rudolf Bultmann, *Jesus Christ and Mythology* (New York: Scribner's Sons, 1958), 15, 20.

3. Bultmann, *Jesus Christ and Mythology*, 38.

4. Walter C. Kaiser Jr., *The Messiah in the Old Testament* (Grand Rapids, MI: Zondervan, 1995), 117.

5. Charles A. Briggs, *Messianic Prophecy* (New York: Scribner's Sons, 1889), 326.

6. Ellen G. White, *Christ's Object Lessons* (Washington, DC: Review and Herald®, 1941), 39, 40.

7. Otto Piper, "Unchanging Promises: Exodus in the New Testament," *Interpretation* 11, no. 1 (January 1, 1957): 3.

8. See the introduction in Michael G. Hasel, "The Book of Exodus," in *The Andrews Bible Commentary*, ed. Ángel M. Rodríguez (Berrien Springs, MI: Andrews University Press, forthcoming).

9. Gerhard F. Hasel, "The Crisis of the Authority of the Bible as the Word of God," *Journal of the Adventist Theological Society* 1, no. 1 (1990): 33; emphasis in the original.

10. Ellen G. White, *Fundamentals of Christian Education* (Mountain View, CA: Pacific Press®, 1894), 187.

CHAPTER 4

The Bible

The Authoritative Source of Our Theology

The question of authority is perhaps the most fundamental issue facing the church today. In a sense, it is *the* question behind every other theological question. For modern people, however, the notion of authority is not attractive, especially when it comes to religious convictions. Contemporary society has become hostile to the concepts of religious authority and obedience. For many, the prevailing impression is that piety is genuine and legitimate only when it rests on an inward, personal conviction; a conviction that should not be subject to external authorities. This profound suspicion of authority is prevalent today and has been a fundamental human problem since Adam and Eve's fall.

It is axiomatic that a sociological group (for the sake of our discussion, a church) requires an element of authority to maintain its identity and integrity. Otherwise, it is difficult, if not impossible, to resolve internal conflict. Furthermore, without the acceptance of authority, it is difficult to achieve theological unity when facing issues of truth and heresy. The authority dilemma is at the heart of theology's modern crisis, dwarfing all other issues that face Christianity.

The response to the question of authority impacts every area of spiritual existence, and its importance cannot be overestimated. It influences our worship, preaching, mission, theology, and ethics. In short, it touches the foundation of how we live as Christ's disciples. Questions dealing with such wide-ranging issues as abortion, Creation and evolution, homosexuality, the role of reason, the relationship of faith and science, and the issue of submission are affected by our understanding of authority.

The meaning of authority

The English word *authority* is derived from the Latin *auctoritas* and refers to the reputation of persons and their capacity to exercise influence.[1] Authority stems from the recognition of someone's superior excellence in a given sphere. Thus, when we speak about the authority of Scripture, we express the idea that the Bible has the superior right to command us what to do, to exact obedience, and to determine and judge the validity and rightness of our faith and practice.[2]

The question of authority is a complex one.[3] It involves many factors that need consideration. Among the various elements involved are the place and role of God, the Bible, tradition, human reason, experience, culture, and worldviews. Every theological position allocates, consciously or unconsciously, a role for each of these authoritative criteria. Differences arise as a result of the priority assigned to each aspect. In modern society, especially in the West, we live in a secularized and humanistic world where man is the center of attention, which raises the question, Is there an authority higher than man himself?

Biblical authority

In biblical teaching, the source of all authority is not man but God Himself (Romans 13:1; Daniel 4:34; John 19:11). The authority of the Bible is connected to the authority of God and derives its authority from God and His divine revelation. Bible students throughout the centuries have accepted Holy Scripture as God's Written Word of truth. Critics of the Christian faith have perceived the Bible as a thoroughly human book and have long challenged the truthfulness of Scripture, knowing that Scripture must be trustworthy to be authoritative. Others have limited the authority of Scripture to theological questions; the Bible is perceived to be authoritative to teach us the way of salvation, but when it comes to historical and ethical issues, the Bible cannot be trusted. But persistent questions remain. Should the Bible be the final authority in all matters of life and practice? Should the Bible reserve the right to interpret itself? Should scientific and sociocultural forces be allowed to influence the meaning of the Bible?

A careful review of Scripture shows that biblical writers considered it authoritative. They viewed it as God's Word in written form. For the apostle Paul, the Scriptures were "the oracles of God" (Romans 3:2). Therefore, he called them the "Holy Scriptures" (Romans 1:2). For Jesus, Scripture was the Word of God that "cannot be broken" (John 10:35). He repudiated the temptations of the devil with a decisive "It is written" (Matthew 4:4, 7, 10). He explained from all the Scriptures the things concerning Himself (Luke 24:27). For Christ, the Old Testament was true, and He attributed an ultimate and unquestionable authority to the Hebrew Scriptures.[4]

Because the Scriptures come to us as the oracles of God, they carry intrinsic divine authority. Unlike human authority, which often rests on force and coercion, divine authority is rooted in love and evidenced in service and self-denial. The Scriptures speak to us with the same authority as Christ. They open up the love and truth of God. There is a profound parallel, expressed in human language, between Christ, the Word made flesh, and Scripture, the Word of God. The words of the prophets and apostles are not merely human words but the Word of God in human form.

According to the biblical writers, the Spirit of Christ speaks in the words of the prophets and the apostles (1 Peter 1:10–12). Jesus Christ was a true human being, but He also wanted to be acknowledged for what He truly was: the Son of God. Similarly, while Scripture's written words bear the limitations of human language, they nevertheless speak with supreme divine authority. What they proclaim "stands forever" (Isaiah 40:8), "is truth" (John 17:17), "is living and powerful" (Hebrews

4:12), and "cannot be broken" (John 10:35). Therefore, we are warned not to add to His Word (Proverbs 30:6; Revelation 22:18, 19). The Scriptures are given as the Word of God, bearing the divine authority of the one true God, and as such they want to be acknowledged.

The scope and sufficiency of scriptural authority

During the Reformation, Protestant Reformers championed *Sola Scriptura*, breaking the ecclesiastical stranglehold of the Roman Catholic Church on the interpretation and authority of the Bible. No longer were church tradition, philosophy, and papal authority the final word. No longer was the Apocrypha granted the same divine origin and authority as canonical Scripture.

Today, new threats to biblical authority have emerged. In the wake of the Enlightenment's emphasis on omnipotent human reason, liberal theology has demolished all external authorities. Divine revelation is judged by human reason, only allowing the reconfirmation of what can be known through rational reflection on nature. Human reason has become the new norm and authority for biblical truth. For many liberal theologians, "revelation" has morphed into a merely rational reaffirmation of moral truths already available to enlightened reason.[5]

Thus, in liberal Protestant circles, the Catholic teaching office has been replaced by autonomous human reason and has led to a "papacy of scholars" and specialists who are engaged in what has been called "scientific scholarship"—the interpretation of the Bible where the application of historical reason and methodological naturalism are consistently employed.[6] Based on human reason as the final norm and highest authority, "liberal scholars [have] engaged in literary and historical research that questioned traditional authorship, challenged factual reliability, rejected or refashioned divine inspiration, and promoted a relativism destructive to doctrinal and ethical absolutes."[7]

Modern biblical criticism has influenced sincere Christians to limit the authority of Scripture, reducing its role to the core essentials of Christian faith and morality. Whenever the Bible speaks on matters of history or science, its statements are subjected to the criteria of naturalistic historical criticism and a naturalistic philosophy of science. Such an approach precludes any supernatural causality in the realm of nature and the flow of history. This exclusion of the supernatural leads to interpretations that ignore, distort, or deny the biblical writers' claims of the divine origin, authority, and truthfulness of their writings.

Another important element in the modern debate about biblical authority is the issue of Scripture's scope and purpose. According to Paul, the primary purpose of the Bible is to make us "wise for salvation through faith which is in Christ Jesus" (2 Timothy 3:15). The apostle John tells us that these things "are written that you may believe that Jesus is the Christ, the Son of God, and that believing you may have life in His name" (John 20:31). Jesus Himself criticized the Jewish leaders of His day for their tragic failure to grasp this important purpose of Scripture: "You search the Scriptures, for in them you think you have eternal life; and these are they which testify of Me. But you are not willing to come to Me that you may have life" (John 5:39, 40).

The debate about the Bible's scope of authority, however, is not about the spiritual purpose of Scripture. The question is whether the authority of Scripture extends to the entire content of the Bible—that is, to all that Scripture affirms (*tota Scriptura*). Some modern critics of the Bible have reduced the authority of Scripture to matters of salvation, effectively nullifying it altogether. Ellen G. White addressed this issue when she wrote: "Many professed ministers of the gospel do not accept *the whole Bible* as the inspired word. One wise man rejects one portion; another questions another part. They set up their judgment as superior to the word; and the Scripture which they do teach rests upon their own authority. Its divine authenticity is destroyed."[8] The principle that Ellen G. White upheld is that all Scripture is to be received as the Word of God because it speaks with divine authority (Acts 24:14; 2 Timothy 3:16). Although the primary focus of the Bible is on the spiritual realm, its authority cannot be limited by arbitrarily excluding it from other areas of human knowledge, such as history and nature. The Bible itself does not explicitly limit the range of its authority to just spiritual things.[9]

Some claim that the Bible is not a science or history textbook and should not be considered authoritative in those areas of knowledge. While this is true in a technical sense, it amounts to a frontal attack on the authority of the Bible. If the truthfulness of the Creation and historical narratives are rejected or reinterpreted along the lines of naturalistic scientific theories or historical research, then their authority is neutralized. In this regard, neither Jesus, the prophets, nor the apostles ever questioned the historical truth of Scripture or the Genesis record. On the contrary, they affirmed Scripture's truthfulness and divine authority. God and His Word are anchored in His historical acts and prophetic utterances. Discrediting the integrity of Scripture's historical details is the initial step in diminishing the authority of the Bible.

Adventist theology appeals to the divine authority of all of Holy Scripture because it views Scripture as the Written Word of God. The Bible does not merely contain the word of God; it is the Word of God in written form. Its authority is not derived from or located in its material center, Jesus Christ. Rather, the Bible is vested with divine authority because of its supernatural inspiration. For this reason, Jesus refers to Scripture as the norm for His theology: "He who believes in Me, *as the Scripture has said*, out of his heart will flow rivers of living water" (John 7:38; emphasis added).

Scripture has not received its authority from the church nor is it legitimized by the current scientific community or through our human experience. Its credibility is derived from divine inspiration. As such, the Bible is characterized by a sense of truth and spiritual authority. It communicates divine truth in a way that nature and creation cannot adequately accomplish because sin has marred the natural world and because the natural world does not share the quality of inspiration.

The Bible's inherent veracity makes Scripture trustworthy and dependable, bearing witness to God's truth. It is the normative standard (*norma normans*) that rules everything else. In the words of Ellen G. White: "In His word, God has committed to men the knowledge necessary for salvation. The Holy Scriptures are to be accepted as an authoritative, infallible revelation of His will. They are the standard of character, the revealer of doctrines, and the test of experience."[10]

Only the Bible can provide an authentic base for understanding our purpose and our destiny. It reveals God's will, His commandments, His character, and the plan of salvation. Such Scripture has the power to unify peoples and cultures, bringing them into the presence of their Creator and Redeemer God.

---

1. Rolf Schieder, "Authority. II. History and Theology," in *Religion Past and Present: Encyclopedia of Theology and Religion*, ed. Hans Dieter Betz et al. (Leiden: Brill, 2007), 1:519. See also Waldemar Molinski, "Authority," in *Encyclopedia of Theology: The Concise Sacramentum Mundi*, ed. Karl Rahner (New York: Seabury Press, 1975), 61.

2. Cf. H. D. McDonald, "Authority," in *Evangelical Dictionary of Theology*, ed. Walter A. Elwell, 2nd ed. (Grand Rapids, MI: Baker Academic, 2001), 153.

3. On the issue of authority, see Peter M. van Bemmelen, "The Authority of Scripture," in *Understanding Scripture: An Adventist Approach*, ed. George W. Reid (Silver Spring, MD: Biblical Research Institute, 2006), 75–89.

4. See John Wenham, *Christ and the Bible*, 3rd ed. (Grand Rapids, MI: Baker Books, 1994), 16–44.

5. Alister E. McGrath, "Enlightenment," in *The Blackwell Encyclopedia of Modern Christian Thought*, ed. Alister E. McGrath (Oxford: Blackwell, 1993), 152.

6. Cf. Gerhard Maier, *Biblical Hermeneutics* (Wheaton, IL: Crossway Books, 1994), 167, 168; Alvin Plantinga, "Two (or More) Kinds of Scriptural Scholarship," in *"Behind" the Text: History and Biblical Interpretation*, ed. Craig Bartholomew et al. (Grand Rapids, MI: Zondervan, 2003), 19–57.

7. Geoffrey W. Bromiley, "Scripture, Authority of," in *The International Standard Bible Encyclopedia*, ed. Geoffrey W. Bromiley, rev. ed. (Grand Rapids, MI: Eerdmans, 1988), 4:363.

8. Ellen G. White, *Christ's Object Lessons* (Washington, DC: Review and Herald®, 1941), 39; emphasis added.

9. See the excellent discussion in Noel Weeks, *The Sufficiency of Scripture* (Carlisle, PA: Banner of Truth, 1988), 85–90.

10. Ellen G. White, *The Great Controversy* (Mountain View, CA: Pacific Press®, 1950), vii.

By Scripture Alone

Sola Scriptura

Seventh-day Adventists have confirmed the importance of the Bible by staunchly affirming the Reformation principle of *sola Scriptura*—that matters of faith and practice should be decided by Scripture alone. As early as 1847, James White unambiguously stated: "The bible is a perfect, and complete revelation. It is our only rule of faith and practice."[1]

To judge all faith and practice by Scripture alone has been called "the battle-cry" of the Protestant Reformation.[2] In June 1520, a papal bull condemned forty-one of Martin Luther's teachings, accusing him of rejecting all the holy teaching of the church. Defending his position, Luther wrote that "Scripture alone is the true lord and master of all writings and doctrine on earth. If that is not granted, what is Scripture good for? The more we reject it, the more we become satisfied with men's books and human teachers."[3] Later, at an appearance before Emperor Charles V at the Diet of Worms, he declared: "My conscience is captive to the Word of God."[4]

The Reformer's bold stand, the Bible, and the birth of Protestantism share a common history and are closely connected. The Reformation pushed back against the patristic tradition, scholastic philosophy, and papal dominion that were allowed to supersede biblical authority. Today, the struggle continues, and the role of Scripture as the sole standard and final norm in matters of theology is still a central tenet of the Protestant church.

Divine authority of the Old Testament

Of late, however, the *sola Scriptura* principle has received criticism from liberal Protestant theologians as well as from Roman Catholics. Some have questioned the validity of *sola Scriptura* because "no statement in Scripture defines *sola Scriptura*."[5] The Bible, allegedly, contains no evidence to support *sola Scriptura*. As scriptural as it might sound, is it a biblical concept?

It is correct that the phrase *sola Scriptura* does not appear in the Bible. In fact, there was a time when the Bible was not. Some have pointed out that taking a completed Scripture as the starting point of our theology is to automatically place ourselves outside the situation of the biblical writers because the completed Scriptures did not exist until long after the central events.[6] This concern leads these people to the conclusion that *sola Scriptura* cannot be biblical. But this line of thinking is deficient for several reasons. Just because a word or a phrase does not occur in the Bible does not mean the idea or concept is absent. For example, this can be seen with other terms like the word *Trinity* that also is not found in Scripture, and yet Scripture attests the concept of a triune Godhead in many places.

For Christians, it is logical to review the place of Scripture in the life of Christ and the apostles. In the Old Testament, there is already evidence of a canonical, authoritative self-consciousness in the recognition that the Written Word was given by God to rule and direct His people.[7] Written documentation accompanies the covenant relationship between God and His people, and these written words were intended to rule and direct their lives.[8] The Old Testament grew from this root.[9]

The New Testament recognizes the canon we now know as the Old Testament. Both Jesus and the apostles used Old Testament Scripture in a normative, canonical sense. They employed such words as "Scripture" (*graphe*) and expressions such as "the law and the prophets" (Luke 16:16), "it is written" (Luke 19:46),

"God has said" (2 Corinthians 6:16), and "Scripture says" (Romans 9:17). Jesus believed the Old Testament and the teachings of Moses were the Word of God (Mark 7:10–13). He cited David as an inspired writer (Mark 12:36). For Him, the inspired writings of the Old Testament were sacred and authoritative (John 10:35; Luke 16:17).

Similarly, the apostles affirmed that the Old Testament God spoke through the mouth of His prophets (Acts 3:21), that the Holy Scriptures are inspired by God (Acts 1:16; 2 Timothy 3:16), and that what Scripture says, God says (Romans 9:17; Galatians 3:8)! Hence, divine Scripture as truth is accepted (Psalms 12:6; 19:7–9; 119:160).

The New Testament states that Paul served the God of his fathers, "believing all things which are written in the Law and in the Prophets" (Acts 24:14). For him, it was clear that "*whatever* was written in earlier times was written for our instruction, so that through perseverance and the encouragement of the Scriptures we might have hope" (Romans 15:4, NASB; emphasis added).[10] Peter affirmed this principle, saying that "no prophecy was ever made by an act of human will, but men moved by the Holy Spirit spoke from God" (2 Peter 1:21, NASB).

Divine authority of the New Testament

For the New Testament writers, divine authority also marked their messages. Paul believed that the things he spoke were "not in words taught by human wisdom, but in those taught by the Spirit" (1 Corinthians 2:13, NASB). His message was received by the apostolic church "not as the word of men, but for what it really is, the word of God" (1 Thessalonians 2:13, NASB). Without fail, the witness of the New Testament is clear: the apostles' writings were "regarded as trustworthy, accurately representing the divine message," and they carried divine authority and had the power to settle controversial issues.[11]

Furthermore, there is a belief that the authority of the New Testament writings is on par with that of the Old Testament.[12] First Timothy 5:18 demonstrates this conviction. Paul says that "the Scripture says, 'You shall not muzzle an ox while it treads out the grain,' and, 'The laborer is worthy of his wages.' " The first part of this verse is a quote from Deuteronomy 25:4, and the second portion is from Luke 10:7. Similarly, Peter refers to the writings of Paul as Scripture (2 Peter 3:16), and the apostles collectively expected their message to be ratified or rejected based on existing Scripture.[13]

The Christians in Berea were commended for "examining the Scriptures daily to see whether these things were so" (Acts 17:11, NASB). They eagerly tested the apostles' witness by implementing the Old Testament test: "To the law and to the testimony! If they do not speak according to this word, it is because they have no dawn" (Isaiah 8:20, NASB). Alluding to this principle, the apostle Paul exhorted the Christians in Corinth "not to exceed what is written" (1 Corinthians 4:6, NASB; cf. 14:37).

Across the board, Christ and the apostles appealed to the authority of existing Scripture with "it is written" (Matthew 4:4–10; Acts 23:5; Romans 3:4, 10; etc.). They firmly established that all of life is to be judged by the Scriptures. The principle of Scripture being the final norm is thus firmly established by Jesus and the apostles and is derived from Scripture itself. Expecting them to state *sola Scriptura* more explicitly fails to account for their historical context and the growth of Scripture. It ignores the fact that Jesus and the New Testament writers used the existing scriptures of the Old Testament as authoritative and considered them on par with the writings of the New Testament.[14]

Still an authority

For Protestants, the principle of *sola Scriptura* is crucially important. However, the idea of *sola Scriptura* has been challenged by some who have converted from Protestantism to Roman Catholicism.[15] It is claimed that Scripture alone cannot be the authoritative final norm for theology because the Bible has produced conflicting interpretations. Is *sola Scriptura* the "sin of the Reformation,"[16] as Stanley Hauerwas contends, because it lacks an objective means to interpret Scripture and leads to extreme individualism? This pervasive interpretive pluralism, it is claimed, constitutes a debilitating problem for any Christian who affirms to go by Scripture alone.[17] In light of this interpretive challenge an increasing number of Protestant and Catholic theologians have advocated a greater authoritative role of the church or tradition and the creeds as integral to a proper understanding of *sola Scriptura*.[18]

But this raises crucial and important questions. Historically, Christians have never universally accepted a creed. Even a cursory reading of the church fathers reveals that there was never a uniform and monolithic Christian tradition, which raises the question: "which of the traditions of the first few centuries of Christianity" should be normative? And no creed has been universally accepted by all Christians. Which poses the question: which church and which tradition should be given prominence in interpreting Scripture? Does not tradition itself stand in need of interpretation? How can Scripture be a final authority if its correct interpretation depends on the church and tradition?

Furthermore, among denominations who affirm Scripture alone as the final norm of their theology, there is impressive harmony on significant biblical teachings, demonstrating that *sola Scriptura* is hardly responsible for discord among Christians. On the contrary, interpretative pluralism is not the problem of Scripture; it is a problem of disparate human minds and faulty presuppositions. (This issue will be discussed in the next chapter.)

The appeal to Scripture alone is nonsensical if Scripture carries no authority, is not needed for our knowledge of God's truth, is unclear in its meaning, or is insufficient in terms of divine intent.[19] What is clear from this study is that adherence to the Word of God remains an ongoing challenge for God's people. They must be sure "to maintain the Bible, and the Bible only, as the standard of all doctrines and the basis of all reforms. The opinions of learned men, the deductions of science, the creeds or decisions of ecclesiastical councils, as numerous and discordant as are the churches which they represent, the voice of the majority—not one or all of these should be regarded as evidence for or against any point of religious faith. Before accepting any doctrine or precept, we should demand a plain 'Thus saith the Lord' in its support."[20]

---

1. James White, Joseph Bates, and Ellen G. White, *A Word to the "Little Flock"* (1847; repr., Washington, DC: Review and Herald®, 1944), 13.

2. Gerhard Ebeling, " '*Sola Scriptura*' and Tradition," in *The Word of God and Tradition: Historical Studies Interpreting the Divisions of Christianity,* trans. S. H. Hooke (Philadelphia: Fortress Press, 1968), 102. Graham Cole calls it the great "catch cry" of the Protestant Reformation. Graham Cole, "*Sola Scriptura*: Some Historical and Contemporary Perspectives," *Churchman* 104, no. 1 (1990): 28.

3. Martin Luther, *Luther's Works,* vol. 32, *Career of the Reformer 2,* ed. George W. Forell (Philadelphia: Fortress Press, 1999), 11, 12.

4. Martin Luther, quoted in Roland H. Bainton, *Here I Stand: A Life of Martin Luther* (Nashville, TN: Abingdon Press, 1950), 185.

5. Robert A. Sungenis, "Point/Counterpoint: Protestant Objections and Catholic Answers," in *Not by Scripture Alone: A Catholic Critique of the Protestant Doctrine of* Sola Scriptura (Santa Barbara, CA: Queenship, 1997), 212. Similarly, John Whiteford, Sola Scriptura: *An Orthodox Analysis of the Cornerstone of Reformation Theology* (Chesterton, IN: Ancient Faith, 1996). More recently, it has been claimed that the occurrence of the term *sola Scriptura* is a rather late invention of nineteenth-century Lutheran theology and that it is not characteristic for Reformed theology. Henk van den Belt, "The Problematic Character of *Sola Scriptura*," in Sola Scriptura: *Biblical and Theological Perspectives on Scripture, Authority, and Hermeneutics,* ed. Hans Burger, Arnold Huijgen, and Eric Peels (Leiden: Brill, 2018), 38–55.

6. James Barr, *Holy Scripture: Canon, Authority, Criticism* (Philadelphia: Westminster Press, 1983), 3. Thus, for Barr, "In the Bible faith was not controlled by scripture: rather scripture derived from faith," 4. Elsewhere, Barr has denied the possibility of formulating a view of Scripture from Scripture itself. He claims, "There is no such thing as 'the Bible's view of itself' from which a fully authoritative answer to these questions can be obtained." James Barr, *Fundamentalism* (London: SCM, 1977), 78. For a sustained response to Barr's sharp criticism and a balanced account of the evidence Scripture provides on this issue, see the discussion in Sinclair B. Ferguson, "How Does the Bible Look at Itself?" in *Inerrancy and Hermeneutic: A Tradition, a Challenge, a Debate,* ed. Harvie M. Conn (Grand Rapids, MI: Baker Books, 1988), 47–66; repr. Peter A. Lillback and Richard B. Gaffin Jr., eds., *Thy Word Is Still Truth: Essential Writings on the Doctrine of Scripture From the Reformation to Today* (Phillipsburg, NJ: P & R Publishing, 2013), 1207–1222. See also John M. Frame, "Scripture Speaks for Itself," in *God's Inerrant Word,* ed. John Warwick Montgomery (Grand Rapids, MI: Bethany Fellowship, 1974), 178–200; repr. John M. Frame, appendix F in *The Doctrine of the Word of God* (Phillipsburg, NJ: P & R Publishing, 2010), 440–462; repr. Lillback and Gaffin, *Thy Word Is Still Truth,* 1224–1241. And finally, see Wayne A. Grudem, "Scripture's Self-Attestation and the Problem of Formulating a Doctrine of Scripture," in *Scripture and Truth,* ed. D. A. Carson and John D. Woodbridge (Grand Rapids, MI: Zondervan, 1983), 19–59.

7. Here we follow the argument that is ably set forth in Ferguson, "How Does the Bible," 50–54.

8. Exodus 17:14; Deuteronomy 5:22, 32; 6:4–8; 29:9; 30:9, 10, 15, 16; 31:24–29; Joshua 1:7, 8; 8:34; 1 Kings 2:3; Nehemiah 8:8–18; 9:3; Jeremiah 30:2; cf. Deuteronomy 4:2. See John C. Peckham, *Canonical Theology: The Biblical Canon, Sola Scriptura, and Theological Method* (Grand Rapids, MI: Eerdmans, 2016), 31.

9. See also the discussion in Peckham, *Canonical Theology*, 16–47.

10. Cf. the parallelism between Romans 15:4 and 5; the perseverance and the encouragement of Scripture are parallel to the perseverance and the encouragement of God!

11. Richard M. Davidson, "Who Is the Author of the Bible?" in *Interpreting Scripture: Bible Questions and Answers*, ed. Gerhard Pfandl (Silver Spring, MD: Biblical Research Institute, 2010), 3. Jesus referred back to Scripture to refute the temptations of the devil!

12. For instance, John introduces quotations from the Old Testament with the words "it is written" (John 6:31; 8:17; 12:14; etc.). It is a phrase that puts to an end all contradiction and expresses the authority of what is being quoted. See Ferguson, "How Does the Bible," 51. Yet a similar expression—"these are written"—marks the end of John's own Gospel (John 20:31). Here the verb *graphō* (write) seems to retain its quasi-authoritative sense (cf. Pilate's words: "What I have written, I have written" [John 19:22]). The letters of the apostles were read not only by the church but alongside the sacred writings of the Old Testament (Colossians 4:16). In the book of Revelation, readers are promised blessings and warned not to add anything or take away anything (Revelation 22:18, 19). This seems to echo the warning in the Old Testament (Deuteronomy 4:2). The book of Revelation seems to claim the same authority that is assumed by the Old Testament itself.

13. Cf. Peckham, *Canonical Theology*, 148.

14. This has been pointed out by Peckham in the excellent chapter "*Sola Scriptura: reductio ad absurdum?*" in *Canonical Theology*, 147.

15. Christian Smith, *The Bible Made Impossible: Why Biblicism Is Not a Truly Evangelical Reading of Scripture* (Grand Rapids, MI: Brazos Press, 2012); Klaus Berger, "Bis der Notarzt kommt: Zurück zur Bibel? Der Ökumenismus treibt neue, welke Blüten," *Frankfurter Allgemeine Zeitung,* September 14, 2004, 33.

16. Stanley Hauerwas, *Unleashing the Scripture: Freeing the Bible From Captivity to America* (Nashville, TN: Abingdon, 1993), 155, quoted in Peckham, *Canonical Theology*, 159.

17. So Smith, *The Bible Made Impossible*, xi and passim..

18. Richard Bauckham has stated that "there has been a narrowing of the rift between Catholic and Protestant views of the relationship between Scripture and tradition, such that some scholars have spoken of an 'ecumenical convergence'" (Richard Bauckham, "Tradition in Relation to Scripture and Reason" in Scripture, Tradition, and Reason: A Study in the Criteria of Christian Doctrine, ed. Richard Bauckham and Benjamin Drewery (New York: T & T Clark, 2004), 125, as quoted in Peckham, Canonical Theology, 151-152.20. Peckham, *Canonical Theology*, 152.

19. Cf. Cole, "*Sola Scriptura*," 24.

20. Ellen G. White, *The Great Controversy* (Mountain View, CA: Pacific Press®, 1911), 595.

Why Is Interpretation Needed?

Have you ever wondered why it is that virtually no theologians and Christian churches exist that do their work without the Bible? They all claim to base their theology on the Bible—and yet they come to fundamentally different conclusions. It is impossible to talk about God and the Christian faith without referencing the Bible. Surprisingly, though commentators and organizations share a scriptural foundation, they often arrive at different conclusions, explaining the host of denominations under the umbrella of Christianity. In part, this is the case because not all theologians and churches are willing to abide by Scripture alone. Other sources are allowed to be authoritative. Reason, experience, and tradition creep in, influencing the interpretation of the Bible and theological conclusions. But even believers who claim *sola Scriptura*, taking the Bible just as it reads, arrive at different opinions on some issues. Why is this the case? The answer to this question involves the mind and life experience of the reader.

No one approaches the Bible with a blank mind

Everyone, without exception, holds beliefs they presuppose or accept when they come to the task of interpreting the Bible.[1] No one approaches the Bible with a blank mind. Our varied experiences, upbringing, education, training, and opinions influence the task of reading Scripture. It is a truism that total neutrality or absolute objectivity cannot be achieved in our act of interpretation. Any theological reflection always takes place against the background of fundamental presuppositions about the nature of the world and the nature of God. And there are other factors like the impact of the culture in which we live that impact our interpretation of Scripture. This context of the reader, the world from which the reader approaches the text of Scripture, unfortunately is often overlooked. Therefore, we need to take a closer look at it.

Our preunderstanding

A significant influence that can skew our interpretation of Scripture and lead us away from the meaning of the biblical text is something called *preunderstanding*.[2] By this, we mean that preconceived notions and understandings are brought to the text *before* the detailed study takes place. Consciously or subconsciously, these preunderstandings are always at work and include "specific experiences and previous encounters with the text that tend to make us assume that we already understand it."[3] Preunderstanding includes all you have heard "at church, in Bible studies, and in your private reading of the Bible. However, preunderstandings of biblical texts are also formed by hymns and other Christian music, pop songs, jokes, art, and nonbiblical literature, both Christian and secular. Likewise, culture constantly creeps in."[4]

The difficulty with preunderstandings is that some can be accurate and others inaccurate. Thus, while a preunderstanding of any given passage may be correct, it is without foundation if the biblical text has not been carefully and thoughtfully studied. It is dangerous to assume that a preunderstanding is always right. The quest for truth requires great humility because human nature naturally defaults to self-confidence. This self-confidence, or pride, is a corrupting influence on the interpreter because "it encourages us to think that we have got the correct meaning before we have made the appropriate effort to recover it. Pride typically does not wait to listen; it knows."[5]

Pride elevates a reader's opinion above the Word of God, and in a bewildering twist, "it is possible to take pride in one's skepticism as well as in one's certainty."[6] Pride, at its ugliest, leads not to humility but to humiliation and ridiculing the biblical text.[7]

The evil twin of interpretive pride is interpretive sloth. It ignores the reader's freedom and responsibility and relies on others—a television preacher, a teacher, a commentary, and even the Spirit—to tell the reader what the text means. It leads the reader to forgo the effort of carefully attending to the text itself.[8]

In contrast to pride that does not want to listen or laziness that listens uncritically, simply absorbing the thoughts of others, our knowledge must be tempered by humility.[9] The attitude of humility is a willingness to submit one's belief to a higher authority. It embraces the conviction that God and His Word are greater than human reason and our current understanding. We must be willing to allow the biblical text to shape and reshape our preunderstandings so that our thinking—and doing—is aligned increasingly with the biblical perspective.

Standing over the Word rather than understanding the Word

Approaching the text with a predetermined theological agenda is another danger of preunderstanding. It brings conclusions to the study of God's Word rather than allowing research to shape the findings. This human tendency calls for openness, honesty, and prayerful seeking to avoid standing *over and above* the Word of God. It also calls for a determination to deliberately place ourselves *under* the Word of God; we must be willing to let the Bible shape our thoughts and understanding. Along this line, Ellen G. White offers this advice:

> In your study of the Word, lay at the door of investigation your preconceived opinions and your hereditary and cultivated ideas. You will never reach the truth if you study the Scriptures to vindicate your own ideas. Leave these at the door, and with a contrite heart go in to hear what the Lord has to say to you. . . .

Do not read the Word in the light of former opinions; but, with a mind free from prejudice, search it carefully and prayerfully. If, as you read, conviction comes, and you see that your cherished opinions are not in harmony with the Word, do not try to make the Word fit these opinions. Make your opinions fit the Word. Do not allow what you have believed or practiced in the past to control your understanding.[10]

Without such openness and honesty no correction of one's preunderstanding is possible. Our presuppositions and our preunderstanding must be modified and reshaped by the text of Holy Scripture and remain under the control of the Bible itself. Rather than being confined by a hermeneutical circle, where we read into Scripture what we bring to Scripture we could speak of a hermeneutical spiral, where our understanding of the Bible is increasingly reshaped and broadened by reading Scripture. The successive exposure to God's Word, through which the interpreter is able to bring his or her preunderstanding in ever closer alignment with biblical truth, enables the biblical interpreter to increasingly think with the biblical text rather than just about the text of the Bible. Thus, God Himself, through the Bible and the Holy Spirit, creates in the interpreter the necessary presuppositions and essential perspective for a proper understanding of Scripture.[11]

The Bible consistently demonstrates that people are not so captive to their preunderstandings that they cannot be transformed. At Thessalonica, for example, Paul "reasoned with them from the Scriptures, explaining and proving that the Messiah had to suffer and rise from the dead" (Acts 17:2, 3, NIV). As a result, "some of the Jews were persuaded and joined Paul and Silas, as did a large number of God-fearing Greeks and quite a few prominent women" (verse 4, NIV).

False familiarity with the Word
Another related danger is that of false familiarity with the Word. It is excellent and praiseworthy to be intimately familiar

with the Bible's content, but if we think we know the story, we no longer read it with attentive eyes and are tempted to forgo careful study. Because of this, some oft-quoted and familiar Bible passages have lost their real meaning. For instance, when speaking about the blessings of two or three who are gathered at a prayer meeting, we often quote Jesus' words: "For where two or three are gathered together in My name, I am there in the midst of them" (Matthew 18:20). While it is a blessing to have Jesus in our midst, this text is not referencing a modern prayer meeting. A careful and attentive reading of the original context shows that He is talking about restoring a brother to fellowship. Following the steps He previously outlined (verses 15–18) will bring His presence and blessing. Whenever this model of reconciliation is followed, regardless of the number of people involved, He has promised to be present!

The challenge of culture influencing our interpretation of Scripture

One of the most potent elements that shapes preunderstanding is culture. "Culture is a combination of family and national heritage. You learned it from your Mom at breakfast, from the kids on the playground at school, and from YouTube. It is a mix of language, customs, stories, movies, jokes, literature, and national habits."[12] Your family background also shapes your cultural world. From our families, for better or for worse, we inherit many of our values, ideas, and images. If you grew up with an abusive father, the biblical picture of God as a loving father will be challenging to you. In this case, the baggage of your family background makes it difficult to understand the biblical truth about God. This baggage, however, does not mean it is impossible for the abused to grasp the true meaning of biblical truth, "but it does mean that they will have to work harder to overcome some of the negative images from their childhood."[13]

Similarly, the automatic images and responses to which we are accustomed present challenges to adequately understanding biblical passages. For example, Paul admonishes us in

Romans 13:1–7 to be subject to the governing authorities. What does this mean if you are situated in a peaceful democracy? What if you are living under the autocratic rule of a despotic ruler? The American authors of a recent textbook on hermeneutics have used this passage to raise the following questions (targeted primarily at American readers): "With this passage in mind, would it have been wrong for you to participate in the Boston Tea Party of 1773? In protest of a new tax on tea, American 'patriots' dumped tons of someone else's tea into the Boston Harbor. Was that a Christian thing to do?"[14] Or to raise the even more significant question: "Was the American Revolution undertaken in disobedience to Romans 13:1–7? Keep in mind that the Revolution was more about economics than about religious freedom. Remember too that when Paul wrote Romans, the government in Rome was much more oppressive and tyrannical than the British government under King George III ever was. What do you think?"[15]

While this example is posed by American authors and aimed at American sentiments, it nevertheless illustrates an interesting point. We rarely question the morality of our native culture. It is routinely presented as wonderful and glorious. But no culture, no matter how loved, is neutral and without fault. If we start our interpretation of the biblical text (in this case, Romans 13:1–7) with the preconceived conclusion "that it *cannot* be critical of the Revolution, we are then placing our culture above the Bible."[16] The uncomfortable challenge we face is allowing the Bible to critique even our culture, not vice versa. After all, we are first and foremost citizens of God's kingdom and have pledged to follow Him and His teachings.

Two mistakes in interpretation

In light of the fact that the Bible was written in a different culture and originated in a different time and place it is obvious that we cannot avoid interpretation. We must work hard to avoid the pitfalls of preunderstanding, presuppositions, and cultural bias. By avoiding two fundamental mistakes, our hard work will be rewarded.

Why Is Interpretation Needed?

The first mistake is to approach the Bible with the wrong method, interpreting the Bible as if God did not exist. Where Scripture is not allowed to supply the categories and parameters for its own method it is interpreted with a foreign worldview. A wrong method inevitably leads to faulty conclusions and a wrong interpretation of its content. The second mistake to be avoided involves the right method employed in the wrong way: using *sola Scriptura* but using it inconsistently. The Bible must be allowed to reconfigure all of our preunderstandings. Submitting to this method of Bible study will bring light and understanding to the humble seeker of truth.

Coming to terms with ourselves takes determination and a willingness to submit to Scripture, allowing the Bible to function as a unifying bond. Through His Word, God will accomplish His work of uniting our theology, hearts, and minds.

---

1. On the important role of presuppositions in the task of interpretation, see Frank M. Hasel, "Presuppositions in the Interpretation of Scripture," in *Understanding Scripture: An Adventist Approach*, ed. George W. Reid (Silver Spring, MD: Biblical Research Institute, 2005), 27–46.

2. Here we follow the excellent discussion about preunderstanding in J. Scott Duvall and J. Daniel Hays, *Grasping God's Word: A Hands-On Approach to Reading, Interpreting, and Applying the Bible*, 3rd ed. (Grand Rapids, MI: Zondervan, 2012), 137–146, esp. 139–144.

3. Duvall and Hays, *Grasping God's Word*, 139.

4. Duvall and Hays, 139.

5. Kevin J. Vanhoozer, *Is There a Meaning in This Text? The Bible, the Reader, and the Morality of Literary Knowledge* (Grand Rapids, MI: Zondervan, 1998), 462.

6. Vanhoozer, *Is There a Meaning in This Text?*, 463.

7. Vanhoozer, 463.

8. Vanhoozer, 463.

9. On the importance of humility, see Hasel, "Presuppositions," 34, 35.

10. Ellen G. White, *Messages to Young People* (Nashville, TN: Southern Publishing, 1930), 260.

11. Cf. Gerhard F. Hasel, *Understanding the Living Word of God* (Mountain View, CA: Pacific Press®, 1980), 77, 78.

12. Duvall and Hays, *Grasping God's Word*, 141.

13. Duvall and Hays, 142.

14. Duvall and Hays, 143.

15. Duvall and Hays, 143.

16. Duvall and Hays, 144; emphasis in the original.

Language, Text, and Context

Words have power. They can rouse people from disobedience to faithful allegiance. At a pivotal point in Israel's history, Joshua urged God's people to action: "Choose for yourselves this day whom you will serve, whether the gods which your fathers served that were on the other side of the River, or the gods of the Amorites, in whose land you dwell. But as for me and my house, we will serve the LORD" (Joshua 24:15). These powerful words shaped the course of a nation and kept Israel in the center of God's plan. However, words can also wreak havoc when used to deceive and destroy. Centuries earlier in the Garden of Eden, Satan lured Eve with the deceptive line, "Has God indeed said, 'You shall not eat of every tree of the garden'?" (Genesis 3:1).

After Adam and Eve fell to Satan's temptation, God continued to communicate with humankind. Prophets and writers recorded the history and theology of Creation, the Fall, the plan of redemption, and the promise of restoration. Writing in Hebrew, Aramaic, and Greek, they used languages unfamiliar to most modern readers. For this reason, it is essential to understand how translation affects our understanding today. Biblical words are packed with significance and often have a range of meaning based on their context. A sentence, a chapter, a book of the Bible, or possibly the whole of Scripture can influence the specific meaning of a text. Understanding these nuances in the original languages clarifies and enriches the message of the Bible. By way of example, the following study of Scripture's remnant concept will demonstrate how meaning can be derived from the broader context of the Bible.

Word studies and semantic range

Word studies are essential in the quest to understand scriptural concepts. This brief study on the remnant theme will illustrate their value. Several key words require examination in an effort to understand the remnant throughout Scripture.[1]

One of the words for remnant is *she'ār*, which means "that which is left over, or remains." In its various derivatives, it occurs 226 times in the Old Testament. The noun form *she'ār* can designate the "remnant" of Israel (Isaiah 10:20) or "His people" (Isaiah 11:11, 16; 28:5). In the latter case, the text indicates this is a remnant chosen by God. Isaiah 4:2–6 and Isaiah 6:13 further describe a holy remnant who have experienced divine judgment.

Other Hebrew words describing the remnant include such terms as *pālat* or *mālat*, "escape";[2] *yāthar*, "to remain over, be left over"; *sārid*, "survivor"; and *'aharît*, "the escape from a mortal threat."[3] The root *pālat* is used eighty times in the Old Testament. In some cases, no escape was possible (Judges 3:29; Jeremiah 32:3, 4), but in many, it was (Genesis 19:17–22; Jeremiah 51:6). Again, in the book of Joel, those who called on the name of the Lord escaped (Joel 2:32).

Another term, *yāthar*, is used 110 times. Often "the rest of the people" (Nehemiah 10:28; 11:1; Haggai 1:12) refers to the remnant that remained in Jerusalem. In some cases, this term is used for a future remnant (Zephaniah 2:9; Zechariah 14:2).[4]

Finally, the words *sārid* and *'aharît* can be found in contexts where a remnant does not survive. In Numbers 24:20, Balaam foretells a time when Amalek would be "last until he perishes," and Amos 9:1 predicts a time in Israel when "he who flees from them shall not get away, and he who escapes from them shall not be delivered." Ezekiel states that Israel's "remnant shall fall by the sword; . . . and your remnant shall be devoured by fire" (Ezekiel 23:25). There is a sense of complete destruction with no remnant surviving.

In the New Testament, the Greek terms *loipós*, "the rest," can be used for those who refuse to repent and harden their hearts. In Romans 11:5, *katáloipoi* is used for the "remnant," and Paul argues that "at this present time there is a remnant according to the election of grace" (Romans 11:5).

The context of these terms indicates that the remnant concept can be described in a variety of ways. Although there is some overlap, these remnant terms generally fall into three categories.

The historical remnant

First, the historical remnant are those people who have escaped a major catastrophe or judgment in a historical context. Tarsee Li writes that the historical "aspect of the remnant motif is applicable regardless of the group's faith or commitment to God."[5] For example, in Genesis 4:1–15, the death of Abel "left only Cain as the progenitor of the human race."[6] Cain's survival was not due to his faithfulness but to the fact that he had murdered his brother.

During Israel's early years in Canaan, a lack of belief in God's promises left a remnant of Canaanites in the Promised Land. This remnant continued to trouble Israel throughout the centuries that followed.

On a different front, Assyrian invasions also troubled Israel. Isaiah 1:4–9 describes a remnant of survivors. They were left due to the circumstances of war, not because of their obedience and faithfulness. These examples of the historical remnant illustrate a remnant that remained because of conditions beyond their control.

The faithful remnant

In addition to the historical remnant, the Bible also speaks of the faithful remnant. They remain faithful to God in both good times and difficult circumstances. Throughout the Bible,

God has a faithful remnant who preserve His will and maintain their witness for Him. They live in history as we all do; however, their characteristics are not shaped by their circumstances but rather by their response to God's calling. Here are three biblical examples of this idea:

1. *Noah.* In Genesis, the Bible records Noah and his family's faithfulness to God's message and mission. "Only Noah was left, and those who were with him in the ark" (Genesis 7:23, ESV).

2. *Joseph.* In Egypt, Joseph assured the salvation of Israel as a remnant through his stalwart service in Potiphar's household, his dedication in the dungeon, and his accurate communication of God's interpretation of dreams. Joseph recognized his role in God's plan: "And God sent me before you to preserve for you a remnant on earth, and to keep alive for you many survivors" (Genesis 45:7, ESV). It has been argued that this "remnant of Joseph" refers to the collective entity that was to perish, but "a remnant, those who returned to Yahweh, would perhaps 'be spared.' "[7]

3. *Daniel.* In Babylon, Daniel and his friends' faithfulness was the means for Nebuchadnezzar's conversion and led to the return of the Judeans to Jerusalem (Daniel 2–4).

At this point, it is worth noting that the faithful remnant might contain some who become unfaithful. Noah and his family were preserved in the ark, but Ham later "saw the nakedness of his father" (Genesis 9:22). Likewise, Lot's family was spared from the destruction of Sodom and Gomorrah, but his wife looked back and became a pillar of salt (Genesis 19:26). This reality requires one to "go beyond the narrow context of the particular passage in which remnant terminology is used to the larger context of the book, or even the entire canon, to determine whether a surviving community in the Bible is a faithful remnant or simply an historical remnant."[8] Overall, this becomes clearer as terms and passages are placed within the wider context of Scripture. It remains true that the Old Testament "has an overarching correlation between the salvation of a remnant and the nucleus of the true people of God."[9]

In the New Testament, Christ's gospel message continues the correlation between the remnant and the true people of God. Jesus' message of salvation, though universal (Mark 1:15), maintained the remnant concept. He came "to seek and to save the lost" (Luke 19:10, NIV) but also suggested that "narrow is the gate and difficult is the way which leads to life, and there are few who find it" (Matthew 7:14). In Matthew 22:14, the chosen are contrasted with those who did not accept Jesus' teachings.

In Romans 9–11, the apostle Paul includes both Jews and Gentiles in the composition of the remnant (Romans 9:24). "This expanded community is possible because of the existence of the faithful remnant of Israel."[10] Thus, the Bible and the early church preserved the concept of a faithful remnant.

The eschatological remnant

The "eschatological remnant" are those who go through the tribulations of the end-time and emerge victorious on the great Day of the Lord to receive His kingdom. This remnant is referenced in Joel's Old Testament prediction: "The sun shall be turned to darkness, and the moon to blood, before the great and terrible day of the LORD comes. And it shall come to pass that all who call upon the name of the LORD shall be delivered; for in Mount Zion and in Jerusalem there shall be those who escape, as the LORD has said, and among the survivors shall be those whom the LORD calls" (Joel 2:31, 32, RSV).

In Revelation 12, Satan, the dragon, is enraged at the woman, the church, and makes "war with the rest of her offspring, who keep the commandments of God and have the testimony of Jesus" (verse 17). Revelation 14:12 contains a similar phrase: "Here is the patience of the saints; here are those who keep the commandments of God and the faith of Jesus."

Interestingly, the term *entolē*, "commandment," occurs in

both of these passages. Does this term mean the Ten Commandments, or is it a more general designation? Johannes Kovar points to contextual arguments in favor of the Ten Commandments. The context of Revelation 12–14 is couched, or embedded, in temple settings. Revelation 11:19 refers to the ark of the covenant being in the Most Holy Place. The second vision refers to the "temple of the tabernacle [tent] of the testimony in heaven" (Revelation 15:5). (The "tent of the testimony" usually refers to the place where the commandments were held.) These verses bracket or "form a kind of *inclusio* around chapters 12–14, with the intent of turning the reader's attention to what was inside the inner compartment of the temple, more specifically, to the ark of the covenant."[11]

Thus, the issue of the Ten Commandments becomes even more pronounced and explicit in Revelation 12:17 and 14:12. The immediate context points to the interpretation that these commandments refer to the Ten Commandments. Also drawing a comparison with Daniel 7, Kovar notes the shift from the little horn's power "changing" laws in Daniel to Revelation's emphasis on a people keeping the law of God.[12] Context makes it clear, and Revelation 12–14 twice notes a description of a people keeping "the commandments of God."

Now, it is important to observe the connection and continuity between the faithful remnant and the eschatological remnant: both are obedient to God's commands. This obedience is not based on their own merits but on the power and strength of Jesus, by whom they are able to achieve righteousness by faith. The significance of a commandment-keeping people at the end of earth's history, at the climax of the great controversy between Christ and Satan, is manifested in Revelation 14 in the first angel's message. This message points people to the hour of God's judgment and directs them to the Ten Commandments—the fourth one in particular: "Then I saw another angel flying in the midst of heaven, having the everlasting gospel to preach to those who dwell on the earth—to every nation, tribe, tongue, and people—saying with a loud voice, 'Fear God and give glory to Him, for the hour of His judgment has come; and worship Him who made heaven and earth, the sea and springs of water' " (Revelation 14:6, 7). John is clearly highlighting God's creative power and identifying the hallmark of His creative work—the seventh-day Sabbath.

The characteristics of the eschatological remnant

In defining the people of the eschatological remnant, we must understand their twofold description in Daniel and Revelation: who they are and when they appear in history. (The present chapter focuses on who they are and their characteristics. In chapter 11, we will focus on when they appear in history and their prophetic timing.)

A review of the apocalyptic prophecies of Daniel and Revelation offers clues about the characteristics of the remnant.

1. The remnant, designated as the 144,000 in Revelation 14, follow the Lamb wherever He goes (verses 1, 4). They follow the example of Christ, rejecting the latest intellectual fads, fashion crazes, and worldly ambition.
2. "In their mouth no lie was found" (verse 5, ESV); instead, they have the truth and proclaim it in the three angels' messages of Revelation 14. They are pure in thought and focused on Christ.
3. The remnant are persecuted for their faith. In Revelation 12, they are identified as "the remnant of her seed" (verse 17, KJV)—that is, the remnant of the woman who battles against the dragon. The little horn makes war on the saints and prevails against them (Daniel 7:21), seeking to destroy the mighty and the people of God (Daniel 8:24). But a remnant will prevail when Michael stands up.
4. The remnant people keep the commandments of God. They are not faithful to only some commandments—but to all of them, including the seventh-day Sabbath which is emphasized in the First Angel's Message (Revelation 14:7) and in the message to Laodicea (Revelation 3:14). In Daniel, the little-horn

power thinks "to change times and law" (Daniel 7:25) and desecrates the sanctuary (Daniel 8:13). Through all of this, the remnant people emerge with the seal of God.

5. "It is these who have not defiled themselves with women, for they are chaste" (Revelation 14:4, RSV). These believers are sober-minded and focused; they are pure in action and thought.

6. The remnant are those whose "deeds follow them" (verse 13, RSV). The remnant are tested through the intense end-time conflict, and their acts or "deeds" are counted to them as righteousness (Hebrews 11:8–10). Just as Abram believed and set out in faith to go where God would lead him, the remnant will have experienced a perfect obedience of following Christ spiritually to the true Land of Promise.

To live such a life before Jesus comes has been seen by some as legalistic and impossible. As a result, in recent years, the Adventist Church has received increased criticism for the doctrine of the remnant, both from within and from without.[13] Some have advocated that this teaching is exclusivist and even elitist.[14] Others have upheld the biblical prophetic and apocalyptic identity of the remnant as we have described it in this chapter.[15]

Of course, the life of the remnant is a divine and supernatural accomplishment; it is a gift from God. It is a humble yearning to follow Jesus, to seek, to save the lost, to warn them of confusion, and to lead them to the light. It is imploring the lost, as Noah once did, to accept salvation and avoid the imminent destruction of the earth. It is a sincere desire to know Jesus and understand His will, treasuring this experience over anything else the world can offer. The desire of the biblical remnant is to remain faithful in all things until He comes.

The idea of the remnant is deeply woven into the words of Scripture. Together, these words contribute to an understanding of the end-time faithful in the Bible's context. Through careful study, the concept emerges, and the student begins to understand the overall theme of the remnant.[16] "The biblical concept of a visible end-time remnant provides Seventh-day Adventists with a more distinct understanding of the nature of the church than is present in any other Protestant church. Adventists believe that the church is not essentially invisible, but rather that it is a reality represented worldwide and inclusive of all nations, peoples, and tongues."[17] In these final days, it is the privilege of every end-time believer to join the remnant church in its mission to proclaim God's message of salvation to a dying world.

---

1. On these terms, see the studies by Gerhard F. Hasel, *The Remnant: The History and Theology of the Remnant Idea From Genesis to Isaiah* (Berrien Springs, MI: Andrews University Press, 1980); Gerhard F. Hasel, "Remnant," in *The International Standard Bible Encyclopedia*, vol. 4, rev. ed., ed. Geoffrey W. Bromiley (Grand Rapids, MI: Eerdmans, 1988), 131–134.

2. Gerhard F. Hasel, "pālat," in *Theological Dictionary of the Old Testament*, vol. 11, ed. G. J. Botterweck, H. Ringgren, and Heinz-Joseph Fabry (Grand Rapids, MI: Eerdmans, 2001), 551–567.

3. Gerhard F. Hasel, " 'Remnant' as a Meaning of 'Ah^arît," in *The Archaeology of Jordan and Other Studies*, ed. Lawrence T. Geraty, Siegfried Horn, and Larry G. Herr (Berrien Springs, MI: Andrews University Press, 1986), 511–524.

4. Gerhard F. Hasel, "Remnant," in *The Interpreter's Dictionary of the Bible*, Supplementary vol., ed. Keith Crim et al. (Nashville, TN: Abingdon, 1976), 735.

5. Tarsee Li, "The Remnant in the Old Testament," in *Toward a Theology of the Remnant*, ed. Ángel M. Rodríguez (Silver Spring, MD: Biblical Research Institute, 2009), 26.

6. Hasel, "Remnant," *International Standard Bible Encyclopedia*, 132.

7. Hasel, *The Remnant: The History*, 203.

8. Li, "Remnant in the Old Testament," 29.

9. Hasel, "Remnant," *Interpreter's Dictionary of the Bible*, 736.

10. Leslie N. Pollard, "The Remnant in Pauline Thought," in Rodríguez, *Toward a Theology of the Remnant*, 80.

11. Johannes Kovar, "The Remnant and God's Commandments: Revelation 12:17," in Rodríguez, *Toward a Theology of the Remnant*, 118; emphasis in the original.

12. Kovar, "The Remnant and God's Commandments," 124.

13. For an overview of issues, see Frank M. Hasel, "The Remnant in Contemporary Adventist Theology," in Rodríguez, *Toward a Theology of the Remnant*, 159–180.

14. Some have advocated that "the final remnant gathering may be broader and more extensive than any formal church" and that "we are a prophetic movement and not God's 'true church.' " Jack W. Provonsha, *A Remnant in Crisis* (Hagerstown,

MD: Review and Herald®, 1993), 163, 167. This view takes a rationalistic approach to truth and not a revelational approach. Others have suggested that God has a remnant in every major world religion—an invisible remnant within Buddhism, Hinduism, and Islam—and this remnant will remain until Jesus comes. See references in Hasel, "Remnant in Contemporary Adventist Theology," 166–170.

15. Gerhard F. Hasel, "The Remnant in Scripture and the End Time," *Adventists Affirm,* Fall 1988, 5–12, 64–66; Clifford Goldstein, *The Remnant: Biblical Reality or Wishful Thinking?* (Nampa, ID: Pacific Press®, 1994); Gerhard Pfandl, "The Remnant Church," *Journal of the Adventist Theological Society* 8, nos. 1–2 (1997): 19–27; Gerhard Pfandl, "Identifying Marks of the End-Time Remnant in the Book of Revelation," in Rodríguez, *Toward a Theology of the Remnant,* 139–158.

16. Cf. Gerhard F. Hasel, *Understanding the Living Word of God* (Mountain View, CA: Pacific Press®, 1980), 113–116.

17. Hasel, "Remnant in Contemporary Adventist Theology," 180.

CHAPTER

Creation, Part 1
The Seventh-Day Sabbath

Today, the seventh-day Sabbath is under heavy attack in secular society and in religious communities. For example, global corporations have attempted to change the calendar in many European countries by designating Monday as the first day of the week and Sunday as the seventh day. Also, the recent papal encyclical on climate change, which calls the seventh-day Sabbath "the Jewish Sabbath," encourages the world to observe a day of rest to alleviate global warming.[1] In some Asian countries, there is a six-day workweek from Monday to Saturday, while in some Muslim countries, in deference to Friday as a holy worship day, a Saturday through Thursday six-day workweek is employed. Moreover, Sunday laws have been put in place to protect the "holiness" of the first day of the week. All of these trends undermine the Bible's seventh-day Sabbath.

In the next two chapters, we will focus on two institutions with their foundation in Creation: the seventh-day Sabbath and the sanctity of marriage. Our study, using these institutions as test cases, will apply the principles of hermeneutics that we have learned.

The Sabbath in Genesis
Genesis offers a simple and eloquent description of Creation's

closing day: "And on the seventh day God ended His work which He had done" (Genesis 2:2). Many creationists emphasize God's work during the six days of Creation but neglect to recognize that God's work did not end on the sixth day. It was the Sabbath day that ended His work of Creation. This is why He declared, "The Sabbath was made for man, and not man for the Sabbath" (Mark 2:27). Jesus made this authoritative statement because He created the Sabbath as the eternal sign and seal of God's covenant with His people. The Sabbath was not only for the Hebrew people but for all humanity. The Sabbath is unique. Unlike other measurements of time that were ordained by the relationship of the movements of created celestial bodies governing the year, the month, and the day, and seasons, the seven-day cycle of the week has no foundation in nature. It is based on God's Creation week and its place and significance is founded solely on His Word and example.

Genesis 2:2, 3 goes on to indicate three things Jesus did after He created the Sabbath day. First, He "rested," setting a divine example of His desire to rest with us. Second, He "blessed" the seventh *day*. It was not the principle of rest that God blessed but a specific day that He blessed. In the Creation narrative, animals are blessed (Genesis 1:22), and Adam and Eve are blessed (verse 28), but out of the days of Creation only the seventh day is blessed.

Third, God "sanctified" it (Genesis 2:3) or "made it holy" (verse 3, ESV) The implication is that He set it apart as a designated holy day for communion with His creation. As the Creator, this was His prerogative, not ours. No other day in the Bible receives these designations, only the seventh-day Sabbath.

The Sabbath in the wilderness

The gift of manna in the wilderness served to enhance the greater gift of the Sabbath (Exodus 16:25, 26). The account of this miracle, which occurred before the giving of the Decalogue at Sinai, uses the noun *šabbāt* for the first time. The Lord commands,

"Tomorrow is a Sabbath rest, a holy Sabbath to the LORD." . . .

". . . For the LORD has given you the Sabbath; therefore He gives you on the sixth day bread for two days. Let every man remain in his place; let no man go out of his place on the seventh day." So the people rested on the seventh day (verses 23, 29, 30).

Gathering twice as much manna on Friday, in obedience to God's command, was a weekly reminder of the word of the Lord concerning the Sabbath. If they did not gather twice as much on Friday, there would be nothing for them on the seventh day.[2] In a practical way on a weekly basis through the miracle of manna provided by God, His people were to understand the holiness of the Sabbath (verse 23) and the rest they were to receive from refraining from work (verses 23, 29, 30).

The wilderness experience also provided a testing ground for man's relationship with God. Would humans trust the Lord of the Sabbath or rely on their own desires? When they went out on the Sabbath to collect manna, God rebuked them: "How long do you refuse to keep My commandments and My laws?" (verse 28). Dishonoring the Sabbath day was tantamount to refusing to obey God's laws and commandments that were established at Creation. In particular, the fourth commandment shows that knowledge of the Sabbath predated Israel's wilderness experience and the giving of the Ten Commandments at Sinai.

The Sabbath in the Commandments

God's creative act and relational interest in our lives, embodied in the Sabbath commandment, stands at the center of the Decalogue. His desire for the Sabbath experience is expressed in the fourth and longest commandment, specifying the what, when, how, and why of Sabbath observance (Exodus 20:8–11).

First, God instructs us *what* to do. The call to Sabbath observance carries a double meaning. On the one hand, we are pointed back to Creation week where we are to remember what

God has done in His creative activity. On the other hand, recognizing our tendency to forget, we are cautioned to remember the Sabbath. Sanctified, set apart, blessed, and made holy—the Sabbath, the seventh day of Creation, functions as a special day of worship and an intimate time of communion with the Giver of all life.

Second, the commandment specifies *when* we are to remember: "The seventh day is the Sabbath of the LORD your God" (verse 10). This measurement of time, ordained by the Creator when He established the seven-day cycle of the week, sets aside every seventh day in commemoration of Creation.

Third, the commandment describes *how* we are to keep the Sabbath. We are to do "no work" (verse 10); this is a command to desist and to cease from the daily work activities that occupy our time. The seventh day is reserved for God, leaving six days for work. The command to refrain from work extends to the household. The whole family as well as servants, livestock, and guests are to enjoy the Sabbath peace. All are to rest and, as part of the family of God, enjoy the collective blessing in Jesus.

Finally, the commandment tells us *why* we are to keep the Sabbath. In six days, God "made the heavens and the earth, the sea, and all that is in them, and rested the seventh day" (verse 11). On the first Sabbath, He modeled His desire for the day by spending it with Adam and Eve—the humans created in His image. To this end, "God blessed the seventh day and sanctified it" (Genesis 2:3). From the beginning, He desired a relationship with His creation. The Sabbath heralds this priority by showcasing a God who steps away from the governance of the universe to spend time with His created beings. There is true physical and spiritual restoration in spending time with our Creator.

The Sabbath in the New Testament

Early in His ministry, Christ highlighted His relationship with the Sabbath. "So He came to Nazareth, where He had been brought up. And as His custom was, He went into the synagogue on the Sabbath day, and stood up to read" (Luke 4:16).

Later, Jesus stated, "Do not think that I came to abolish the Law or the Prophets; I did not come to abolish but to fulfill" (Matthew 5:17, NASB). Jesus certainly challenged ideas of Sabbath-keeping among the Jews of His day which had built laws around Sabbath-keeping that made it a burden. His challenges often came in the form of miracles, casting out demons (Mark 1:21–28; Luke 4:33–35) and healing on the Sabbath (Matthew 8:14, 15; Luke 6:6–10; 13:10–17; 14:1–4; John 5:1–9; 9:1–41). Jesus' healing of the paralytic at the pool of Bethesda and His subsequent command to walk "demonstrated the reality and completeness of his [the paralytic's] cure by walking and carrying home the pallet on which he had been lying."[3] Justifying this miraculous healing, Jesus confronted the Pharisees: "Is it lawful on the Sabbath to do good or to do evil, to save life or to kill?" (Mark 3:4).

In Matthew 24:20, Jesus anticipates the destruction of Jerusalem in A.D. 70, urging His listeners to "pray that your flight may not be . . . on the Sabbath." By implication, Jesus affirms the Sabbath and its sacredness even up to A.D. 70.[4] The Sabbath was to be a time of rest, worship, and peaceful reflection on the mighty works of God.

Even in death, Jesus rested in the tomb on the Sabbath, being raised to life on the first day of the week. The women who anointed Jesus for burial "rested on the Sabbath according to the commandment" (Luke 23:56). "The accusative, *to sabaton*, indicates that they rested 'all through the Sabbath.' " Luke is careful to account for the Sabbath in his record of the Passion, referring to three distinct days: "the day of preparation, the Sabbath, and the first day of the week."[5]

In the Gospels, Jesus' example is instructive for today's followers. In the true spirit of the day, He healed and cast out demons, thereby emphasizing the Sabbath as a day of joy, celebration, and freedom from guilt and the burdens of sickness. Never did He speak about abolishing the Sabbath. Instead, He told His disciples, "If you love Me, keep My commandments" (John 14:15).

In the early church, the pattern of Sabbath keeping

continued. The phrase found in Luke 4:16—"as His custom was"—used for Jesus' entrance to the synagogue when He returned to His hometown of Nazareth, is also used of Paul. "They came to Thessalonica, where there was a synagogue of the Jews. Then Paul, as his custom was, went in to them, and for three Sabbaths reasoned with them from the Scriptures, explaining and demonstrating that the Christ had to suffer and rise again from the dead, and saying, 'This Jesus whom I preach to you is the Christ' " (Acts 17:1–3). In Corinth, Paul "reasoned in the synagogue every Sabbath, and persuaded both Jews and Greeks" (Acts 18:4). On his third journey, he arrived at Ephesus and "went into the synagogue and spoke boldly for three months, reasoning and persuading concerning the things of the kingdom of God" (Acts 19:8). Later, he withdrew and entered the school of Tyrannus, after which "all who dwelt in Asia heard the word of the Lord Jesus, both Jews and Greeks" (verse 10).

Portraying Jesus and the apostles as Sabbath keepers is a consistent pattern in the New Testament. Even after Christians left the synagogues, there is no indication they worshiped on a different day. That there was no controversy about the binding nature of the Sabbath is evidenced by the omission of a Sabbath directive from the Jerusalem Council. Apparently, it was a nonissue in the new movement's struggle to integrate Jews and Gentiles. "The silence of the conference on this subject eloquently testifies to the continual observance of the Sabbath by both Jewish and Gentile Christians."[6]

The Sabbath today

Contemporary studies on the Sabbath employ three major approaches to assert that the seventh-day Sabbath is no longer binding: (1) the historical-critical approach; (2) the old covenant–new covenant argument, focusing on ancient Israel in contrast to the church established by Christ; and (3) affirmations of seventh-day Sabbath keeping as biblical in the Old and New Testaments but reassigning it to an eschatological sabbath for all humanity.

The historical-critical approach denies a priori the claim of the authorship of the Pentateuch and would date the Sabbath passages in the first two books of the Bible to later Israelite tradition, various schools (J, E, D, P), or later editors and redactors. For Willy Rordorf, the Jewish Sabbath of Genesis 1–2, Exodus 20, and Deuteronomy 5 "originated after the occupation of Canaan and . . . the evidence is to be found in documents which date from the early monarchical period," but "credit for such an invention has not been given to the Israelites."[7] In this regard, scholars have searched for the origin of the Sabbath outside of Israel, assuming it was borrowed from some other ancient civilization, be it Babylonian, Kenite, Arabic, or Ugaritic. "In spite of the extensive efforts of more than a century of study into extra-Israelite sabbath origins, it is still shrouded in mystery. No hypothesis commands the respect of a scholarly consensus."[8] Could the search for Sabbath origins outside of Scripture be futile because the Sabbath originated at Creation and was ordained by God, who measured the seven-day cycle?

Theologians have also contended that the Sabbath was part of the Israelite or Jewish covenant, which was "annulled" by Jesus in His healings on the Sabbath and replaced in the New Testament with the Lord's Day.[9] They claim this can be traced in the New Testament itself. But as noted above, there is no evidence that Jesus or the apostles changed the Sabbath. Their observance of it as well as their insistence on keeping the commandments testify to the honoring of the Sabbath.

Others have claimed that the Sabbath is part of the ceremonial law but not the moral law.[10] D. A. Carson, among others, anchors the Sabbath not in Genesis but in Exodus 20. In his view, Jesus' Messiahship provides the authority for a new covenant that frees Christians from the Jewish Sabbath to celebrate a new day of Redemption.[11] But as we have seen, both Creation and the gift of manna indicate that the Sabbath was created before Sinai. Some further deny that Sunday was introduced by the Church of Rome. But they ignore the position taken by church fathers like Thomas Aquinas and several recent dissertations that have shown that, "The Church of Rome has been primarily responsible for the institution of Sunday observance."[12] This fact is significant for Protestant Christians who claim to stand on the foundation of Scripture alone (*sola Scriptura*) and not on the traditions and teachings of ecclesiastical councils.

More recently, N. T. Wright has argued that "linear time (which was part of God's good creation) continues, but it is now intersected with a new phenomenon, a new kind of time. . . . So time seems now capable of being telescoped together and then pulled apart again. One might call this 'Spirit-time'. . . . All of this is focused on Jesus Christ."[13] For Wright, "Now that heaven and earth have come together in Jesus Christ, and now that the new day has dawned, we live (from that point of view) in a perpetual sabbath."[14] The Sabbath, as either the seventh day or the first day or any specific day, ceases to exist and becomes part of the Christian "story." Transposed into a principle of rest, the Sabbath is separated from the specific (historic) day that God has designated.

However, uncoupling Sabbath rest from the seventh day has implications for the eschatological nature of the Sabbath and its relation to prophetic last-day events. The Sabbath loses its distinctive character as a divine test and sign of the commandment-keeping remnant (Revelation 12:17; 14:12; cf. Ezekiel 20:12).

Today's challenge is to champion the seventh day of the week as the biblical day of rest, instituted by God at Creation and upheld throughout Scripture. Sabbath keeping that honors the Creator God, Author of the Ten Commandments, is the hallmark of an end-time people who "keep the commandments of God and the faith of Jesus" (Revelation 14:12). Indeed, the Sabbath demonstrates our love and faithfulness, becoming a visible sign that we belong to the only true God.[15]

---

1. Pope Francis, *Laudato Si'* (*Praise Be to You*) (Vatican City: Vatican Press, 2015), § 71, 237.

2. Gerhard F. Hasel, "The Sabbath in the Pentateuch," in *The Sabbath in*

Scripture and History, ed. Kenneth A. Strand (Washington, DC: Review and Herald®, 1982), 26, 27.

3. Walter F. Specht, "The Sabbath in the New Testament," in Strand, *The Sabbath in Scripture and History*, 100.

4. Specht, "The Sabbath in the New Testament," 103.

5. Specht, 105.

6. Specht, 111.

7. Willy Rordorf, *Sunday: The History of the Day of Rest and Worship in the Earliest Centuries of the Christian Church* (Philadelphia: Westminster Press, 1968), 18, 19.

8. Gerhard F. Hasel, "Sabbath," in *Anchor Bible Dictionary*, vol. 5, ed. David Noel Freedman (New York: Doubleday, 1992), 851.

9. Rordorf, *Sunday*, 70, 215, 237; cf. Paul K. Jewett, *The Lord's Day: A Theological Guide to the Christian Day of Worship* (Grand Rapids, MI: Eerdmans, 1972), 16–18.

10. H. M. Riggle, *The Sabbath and the Lord's Day*, 6th ed. (Anderson, IN: Gospel Trumpet, 1928), 148.

11. D. A. Carson, ed., *From Sabbath to Lord's Day: A Biblical, Historical, and Theological Investigation* (Grand Rapids, MI: Zondervan, 1982).

12. Samuele Bacchiocchi, *From Sabbath to Sunday: A Historical Investigation of the Rise of Sunday Observance in Early Christianity* (Rome: Pontifical Gregorian University Press, 1977), 310, 311. Cf. Vincent J. Kelly, *Forbidden Sunday and Feast-Day Occupations* (Washington, DC: Catholic University Press of America, 1943), 2, see John Gilmary Shea, "The Observance of Sunday and Civil Laws for Its Enforcement," *American Catholic Quarterly Review* 8 (January–October 1833): 139: "The Sunday, as a day of the week set apart for the obligatory public worship of Almighty God, . . . is purely a creation of the Catholic Church."

13. N. T. Wright, *Scripture and the Authority of God: How to Read the Bible Today* (New York: HarperCollins, 2011), 162, 163.

14. Wright, *Scripture*, 167.

15. Frank M. Hasel, "What Does It Mean to Be a Seventh-day Adventist? A Short Theological Reflection," *Adventist Review*, May 2019, 49.

Creation, Part 2

Marriage and the Family

The seventh-day Sabbath is a foundational institution established at Creation. The law of the Sabbath is written by God's own finger in stone as the sign by which humanity acknowledges His Creatorship and His sovereignty over their lives throughout the span of earth's history (Rev 12:17; 14:7). It is the fourth, culminating commandment defining and protecting our relationship with Him as expressed in the first table of the decalogue. The next command, the fifth commandment, connects our vertical relationship with God and our horizontal relationship with the rest of humanity. "Honor your father and your mother, that your days may be long upon the land which the LORD your God is giving you" (Exodus 20:12).

These two commandments are unique in two ways. First, they are the only two commandments spoken as a command, with no prohibition. The fourth commandment begins with "remember," and the fifth commandment with "honor." Second, they define our relationships with God and humans by appealing to one's sources of existence. God created humans and granted them the gift of procreation. The fourth commandment is a call to honor God as the Creator, and the fifth commandment is an appeal to honor one's parents as procreators.

Why does God link honoring our parents with exclusive

worship of Him? The answer lies in the first chapter of Genesis. In a small way, God, as the Creator of the universe and Source of all life, has shared with earthly parents the joy of creation. They are partners with God in populating the planet. As such, their position and role in creation deserve honor from their children.

Genesis as foundation

On the sixth day, God reached the climax of Creation—humanity. The plural pronoun for God is used for the first time in Genesis 1:26: "Let Us make man in Our image." All the persons of the triune Godhead, in a loving relationship with Each Other, created the first man and woman. "In the image of God He created him; male and female He created them" (verse 27). First, Adam is created. God then takes a rib from Adam and fashions Eve, drawing this pronouncement from the first man, "This is now bone of my bones and flesh of my flesh" (Genesis 2:23). Adam names her woman.

The first marriage forever established that man and woman were made for each other and set the model for all subsequent marriages. "A man shall leave his father and mother and be joined to his wife, and they shall become one flesh" (verse 24). God could have chosen various ways to populate the earth, but He chose marriage. Why?

Space does not allow for an expansive answer to this question, but in general terms, woman was originally part of man—his very flesh and bone. In marriage, she returned to man, becoming one with him again. The created complementarity of man and woman is a biological fact and naturally provides for their union. God's instructions to the first pair further clarify the purpose of this union: "Then God blessed them, and God said to them, 'Be fruitful and multiply; fill the earth and subdue it'" (Genesis 1:28).

In this way the foundation of humanity and society on earth is defined in God's creative life-giving work in the beginning. The assurance of humanity's future is based on following His design. The human race is to be perpetuated from each father and mother, also a man and woman. The gift of God's marriage union is His final act in the physical creation. The institution of the Sabbath in time brings this union into communion with the divine agent of Creation, Jesus Christ. Our creation in God's image forms the intended identity we have in Jesus Christ and our acknowledgement of identifying with Him comes in our worshiping on His seventh-day Sabbath. The loving relationship of the Creator with the family is to be perpetuated from the husband and wife to their children on through the generations of history. There is a sacred trust given to the nuclear family as the basis for the rest of culture and society. As their relationship with God and with each other goes, so goes earth's history. Perhaps it is for this reason that the fifth commandment, the seventh commandment, and the tenth commandment address the sanctity of marriage in the honor bestowed to parents and ending with the instruction not to covet a neighbor's wife (Exod 20:17).

The internal witness of Scripture

Allowing Scripture to interpret Scripture, let us examine the biblical concept of marriage. The natural order of marriage between a man and a woman is reaffirmed in positive way throughout the Bible:

1. The generations of humankind are traced through the history of marriage (Genesis 5; 11; 1 Chronicles 1–3).
2. The promised Messiah is traced through marriage (Genesis 3:15; Matthew 1:1–17; Luke 3:23–38).
3. Abraham and Sarah are made a great nation through Isaac. The divine promise was fulfilled as a result of their union (Genesis 18:10). The covenant promise given to Abraham and Sarah stands in contrast to the judgment against Sodom and Gomorrah (Genesis 19). Breaking the natural order brought severe consequences to those wicked cities.
4. When the line of the Promised Seed was jeopardized by the death of Ruth's husband during the famine in

Moab, God guided Ruth to Boaz of Bethlehem (the "house of bread"). Through their marriage, Obed was born (Ruth 4:13–17). He became the father of Jesse, who became the father of David. This love story featuring the gift of rekindled love and marriage was a provision for the future promise.

In the New Testament, Jesus and the apostles reaffirm marriage. Notice how Jesus responds to the Pharisees' inquiry about divorce. Quoting from Genesis 2, He says, "Therefore what God has joined together, let not man separate" (Matthew 19:6). Jesus affirms Scripture, and Genesis in particular, by stating that the joining of man and woman was divinely ordained by God and should not be separated by man.

Paul specifically addresses the foundational nature of the Genesis narrative in Romans 1:20–28. Beginning with Creation, he affirms that all humanity, through nature, could come to understand the reality of God's existence. However, he goes on to state that "they exchanged the truth of God for a lie, and worshiped and served the creature rather than the Creator." This choice to believe in a lie led them astray: "For this reason God gave them over to degrading passions," and what follows is a description of same-sex behavior between two females and between two males (Romans 1:25, 26, NASB).

For Paul, biblically defined sexuality between a man and a woman is natural and intrinsic to the nature of human beings created in God's image (Genesis 1:27). Humankind's refusal to accept the Creator, exchanging His worship with that of the creature, causes them to be handed over to their lusts. In this context, sexuality is more than behavior and activity; rather it should be understood within a biblically-defined concept of created humanity in totality that provides the framework to reinforce moral behavior.

Recent trends

Many nations of the world have approved same-sex marriages, overturning previous laws protecting the family structure and compromising the principle of one man and one woman at the center of marriage. This unprecedented development raises new questions about the institution of marriage and the separation of church and state, not to mention the sanctity of marriage and family as defined in Scripture.

For Christians, the pressing question centers on whether marriage is a biblical institution and a biological necessity for the creation of life or a mere personal preference, relegated to the sphere of individual human rights. Is marriage defined by God or by culture and society? Christianity's response to this question has determined the direction of its churches.

Today, same-sex marriage is increasingly accepted by mainstream Protestant churches. In 2009, both the Evangelical Lutheran Church in America and the Episcopal Church in the United States independently voted to approve homosexual clergy.[1] In 2013, Lutherans recently elected a practicing gay bishop in California.[2] The Presbyterian Church (USA) now welcomes practicing homosexuals as ministers and leaders.[3] In Europe, the Scottish Episcopal Church approved same-sex unions in 2017.[4] These developments have caused significant divisions in Protestant denominations and a sharp decline in membership.

And what arguments do traditionally Christian countries use to justify their approval of same-sex marriage? Recent books on the subject indicate that the key issues involve the issue of interpretation in the following areas: (1) a redefinition of Creation and the acceptance of an evolutionary worldview; (2) a reinterpretation of key passages in Scripture that have historically been seen as prohibiting homosexual behavior; and (3) an application of Bible passages on love and acceptance that take precedence over clearer passages on the subject of marriage and sexuality.

Redefining Creation

Those who affirm same-sex relationships have reinterpreted Genesis in several ways. Matthew Vines suggests God needed to provide Adam with a woman because they were the first parents and were required to procreate to fill the earth, implying that this is not a necessity today in our world of overpopulation.[5] He further states that Genesis 2 does not emphasize Adam's and Eve's differences but "their *similarity* as human beings."[6] While Adam does speak of Eve as "bone of my bones and flesh of my flesh," this comparison is in reference to the other species Adam observes (Genesis 2:23). Eve is clearly different. Sameness and companionship were not all that mattered because they later became "one flesh" (verse 24). Here the complementary nature of God's design becomes a key element in making this physically possible. Adam and Eve were a perfect anatomical match for each other. From the beginning, procreation has been the essential purpose for marriage (Genesis 1:27, 28) and even though not all couples can have children, the parental roles of a husband and wife are assumed in the fifth commandment.

Others suggest Genesis is merely descriptive and should not be used to prescribe, or proscribe, modern sexual behavior; it only describes what God did. In this view, He did not make marriage between a man and a woman normative, nor did He exclude other relationships.[7] However, this argument founders on the prescriptive fifth commandment, the Levitical laws, and the New Testament's affirmation of the natural created order.

On the sixth day, saving the best for last, God fashioned man and woman as the apex of Creation: "God saw everything that He had made, and indeed it was very good" (Genesis 1:31). His design was perfect, and there was no need for proscriptive statements. Sadly, after the introduction of sin and man's deviation from God's plan for marriage and family, such statements would be needed.

Redefining other passages on the basis of culture

After the entrance of sin, sexual deviance was addressed by the same author who wrote Genesis: "You shall not lie with a male as with a woman. It is an abomination" (Leviticus 18:22). Again, in Leviticus 20:13, he writes, "If a man lies with a male as he lies with a woman, both of them have committed an abomination. They shall surely be put to death. Their blood shall be upon them."

These commands occur in a series of sexual prohibitions that include adultery, incest, child sacrifice, and bestiality. Each ban is still valid in contemporary society. In this list, only the homosexual act is designated as an abomination (*tôb'ēbâ*); this term is also translated as "an abhorrent thing"—something detestable, loathsome, utterly repugnant, or disgusting.[8] The penalty for this act is death (verse 13), and if that action is not taken, the person is to be expelled from the whole community.[9]

Paul reaffirms the Levitical standard in his New Testament list of sins, including the sexually immoral (or fornicators, *pornoi*), idolaters, adulterers, the effeminate (*malakoi*), homosexuals (*arsenokoitai*), thieves, greedy people, drunkards, verbally abusive people, and swindlers (1 Corinthians 6:9–11; cf. 1 Timothy 1:8–10). Plainly, these sins have no place in faithful Christianity. Nevertheless, the recent agenda to support same-sex marriage has taken the liberty to redefine clear Old and New Testament passages.

In regard to Leviticus 18 and 20, some people have argued that the prohibitions are part of the ceremonial law and, therefore, are not binding in the new covenant. This argument is also used against the seventh-day Sabbath. Others suggest these prohibitions applied only to the Israelites within that time and culture.[10] Some cite the prohibition against wearing mixed fabrics as a Levitical law we do not follow today.[11] "The Levitical enactments . . . characterize it unequivocally as ceremonially unclean rather than inherently evil."[12] Yet this disregards the binding nature of the Genesis Creation order and the fifth commandment.

Moreover, all the prohibitions, within the context of Leviticus 18 and 20, against incest, bestiality, and child sacrifice remain binding in cultures today. Why should homosexuality, noted with even stronger language and consequences, be different? And how does one explain Paul's continued condemnation of this act in the New Testament?

Another approach contends that biblical texts, together

with the Sodom narrative in Genesis 19:1–12, reflect a patriarchal system that is no longer aligned with the New Testament view, much less a modern one. Thus Vines states, "Yes, ancient Israel was dominated by patriarchal structures and norms, which we see reflected throughout the Old Testament—including in its prohibitions of male same-sex intercourse. . . . But far from being a reason to view Scripture as outdated or sexist, the Bible itself is what points us toward a path where patriarchy is no more."[13] Advocates of the trajectory hermeneutic construe Galatians 3:28 as a statement of validation for same-sex relations: "There is neither Jew nor Greek, there is neither slave nor free, there is neither male nor female; for you are all one in Christ Jesus."[14] On this verse, Vines writes, "Paul undermined the belief that patriarchy has a place in the kingdom of God."[15]

Upon closer examination, however, it is fair to ask, Does Galatians 3:28 redefine the image of God's Creation order, or is Paul stating that in Christ *every* person has equal access to the gift of salvation? Does the context support the removal of sexual distinctions, allowing for same-sex relations and marriage? Is Paul pointing to a hermeneutic outside of Scripture? And why would Paul contradict himself, advocating a position he takes nowhere else (Romans 1:21–26; 1 Corinthians 6:9–11; 1 Timothy 1:8–10)?

In Galatians 3:28, Paul is not redefining human sexuality, nor is he introducing a new hermeneutic. Like Jesus in Matthew 19, Paul does the opposite; he unequivocally uses Scripture, repeatedly citing the creative work of God in Genesis. This appeal to origins is the basis of his theology of marriage and the roles of men and women (Romans 1:24–27; 1 Timothy 2:13, 14; 1 Corinthians 11:2–16).

Furthermore, in 1 Corinthians 5:1, 2, Paul commands that a man in an incestuous relationship with his stepmother be disfellowshiped, upholding Leviticus 18 and 20. He does this without asking whether they are engaged in a monogamous and loving relationship. Such a question is irrelevant because, for Paul, the prohibitions in Leviticus that include homosexual acts are taken at face value as normative.[16]

Finally, for Jesus, Paul, and other New Testament writers, the grace of Christ provides the solution to the temptations and tendencies of sin. Jesus said, "These things I have spoken to you, that in Me you may have peace. In the world you will have tribulation; but be of good cheer, I have overcome the world" (John 16:33). Just as in Adam all have sinned and fallen short of the glory of God, so in Christ and His righteousness, all can overcome (Romans 3:23; 5:14–17; 1 John 5:4; Revelation 21:7), putting "on the new man who is renewed in knowledge according to the image of Him who created him" (Colossians 3:10).

It is an honor to identify with Christ and joyfully accept human sexuality as ordained in Eden. Scripture never wavers from the Genesis blueprint, and the mission of an end-time remnant is to fulfill the three angels' messages and to call people out of confusion, back to the Bible, and into the light. By God's grace, each believer who heeds the call will be empowered to "keep the commandments of God and have the testimony of Jesus Christ" (Revelation 12:17).

1. Laurie Goodstein, "Lutherans Offer Warm Welcome to Gay Pastors," *New York Times*, July 25, 2010, https://www.nytimes.com/2010/07/26/us/26lutheran.html.

2. Sarah Pulliam Bailey, "ELCA Lutherans Elect First Openly Gay Bishop," Religion News Service, June 3, 2013, https://religionnews.com/2013/06/03/elca-lutherans-elect-first-openly-gay-bishop/.

3. Goodstein, "Lutherans."

4. Harriet Sherwood, "Scottish Episcopal Church Votes to Allow Same-Sex Weddings," *Guardian*, June 8, 2017, https://www.theguardian.com/world/2017/jun/08/scottish-episcopal-church-votes-to-allow-same-sex-weddings.

5. Matthew Vines, *God and the Gay Christian* (New York: Convergent, 2014), 45–47.

6. Vines, *God and the Gay Christian*, 46; emphasis in the original.

7. John R. Jones, " 'In Christ There Is Neither . . .': Toward the Unity of the Body of Christ," in *Christianity and Homosexuality*, ed. David Ferguson, Fritz Guy, and David Larson (Roseville, CA: Adventist Forum, 2008), pt. 4, 3–42.

8. L. Koehler, W. Baumgartner, and J. J. Stamm, *Hebrew and Aramaic Lexicon to the Old Testament* (Leiden: Brill, 2001). Robert A. J. Gagnon, *The Bible and Homosexual Practice* (Nashville, TN: Abingdon, 2001), 113; see also Robert A. J. Gagnon, "The Scriptural Case for a Male-Female Prerequisite for Sexual

Relations: A Critique of the Arguments of Two Adventist Scholars," in *Homosexuality, Marriage, and the Church: Biblical, Counseling, and Religious Liberty Issues*, ed. Roy E. Gane, Nicholas P. Miller, and H. Peter Swanson (Berrien Springs, MI: Andrews University Press, 2012), 53–161.

9. Gagnon, *The Bible and Homosexual Practice*, 114–117.

10. Jacob Milgrom, *Leviticus 17–22*, Anchor Bible (New York: Doubleday, 2000), 1788.

11. Justin Lee, *Torn: Rescuing the Gospel From the Gays-Vs.-Christians Debate* (New York: Jericho, 2012), 174–176; John Shore, *Unfair: Christians and the LGBT Question* (self-pub., CreateSpace Independent Publishing, 2013), 8.

12. John Boswell, *Christianity, Social Tolerance, and Homosexuality: Gay People in Western Europe From the Beginning of the Christian Era to the Fourteenth Century* (Chicago: University of Chicago Press, 1980), 101, 102.

13. Vines, *God and the Gay Christian*, 93.

14. See Vines, 92, 93; Jones, " 'In Christ,' " pt. 4, 28, 29.

15. Vines, *God and the Gay Christian*, 93; cf. James V. Brownson, *Bible, Gender, Sexuality: Reframing the Church's Debate on Same-Sex Relationships* (Grand Rapids, MI: Eerdmans, 2013), 81.

16. Roy E. Gane, "Some Attempted Alternatives to Timeless Biblical Condemnation of Homosexual Acts," in Gane, Miller, and Swanson, *Homosexuality, Marriage, and the Church*, 167.

CHAPTER

10

The Bible as History

All life is rooted in history. History is the record of man's experience, the fabric of life, and the frame of reference for human identity. We exist and live in time and space. Events and choices shape us, mold us, and create the people we become. This reality is the biblical worldview and explains why Scripture traces God's acts in specific settings over time. Unsurprisingly, geography and its many places—cities, countries, bodies of water, rivers, mountains, nations—are at the core of the biblical narrative.[1]

The scriptural understanding of God's work is also linear and forward moving, not cyclical as in the mythical thinking so prominent among the other conceptions of the ancient world.[2] God is revealed as One who is the beginning, center, end, and eternal future of human history. He inaugurates time "in the beginning" (Genesis 1; 2; John 1) by creating the sun and the moon "for signs and seasons, and for days and years" (Genesis 1:14). He seals His sovereignty as Creator in the perpetual weekly cycle that ends in the seventh-day Sabbath, sanctifying it and making it holy (Genesis 2:1–3).

After the Fall, the divine-human bond is broken, and the plan of redemption is enacted, pointing forward to the promised Messiah. History and prophecy are inextricably linked to

God's plan to save humanity. With intense interest, the onlooking universe follows the events of the great controversy on earth, marveling at God's plan to save humanity.

Through His covenant promise, God works directly with His agents—Adam, Noah, Abraham, Moses, David, and the prophets—to see that history's prophetic destiny of the promised Messiah is fulfilled. In the "fullness of the time," God sends His Son, the ultimate divine act in human history, to pay the penalty for humanity's rebellion against the divine law of God's government (Galatians 4:4). All creation anticipates Christ's proclamation from the cross: "It is finished" (John 19:30). As prophesied, after three days, He breaks free of the tomb, appears to hundreds of people, and ascends to heaven. He then begins His high priesthood in the Holy Place before entering the Most Holy in 1844 for the pre-Advent judgment of the living and the dead. When this judgment is finished, He returns in triumphant glory to claim His ransomed people, fulfilling the promise of Revelation 22:20: "Surely I am coming quickly." The scope of Scripture thus spans the beginning and end of human history. No other sacred religious text provides this perspective of totality in time and place. No other books, secular or sacred, contain prophetic messages of God's omniscient foreknowledge and His intervention in human affairs.

For these reasons history is essential to the interpretation of the Bible. Because the Bible is historically constituted, history (and by extension geography) is the "place," if you will, where God gives humanity an opportunity to test and confirm the truthfulness of His Word. That is why history and historical details are where the trustworthiness of the Bible and of God's Word are challenged the most and where criticism often begins first.

Historie, Geschichte, and salvation history

Since the Enlightenment, the subject of history has become one of the most difficult problems in biblical studies.[3] This is primarily due to the presuppositions of the historical-critical method and its virtual denial of the possibility of divine action in human history. As Walter Dietrich has written, "In the modern age, history must be understood and described *esti deus non deratur* ("as though God did not exist")." At the same time, he admits that this makes it difficult when assessing biblical history. "God plays an active role. . . . God gets personally involved. . . . He sends prophets. . . . He moves events." Dietrich then concludes, "What enlightened person can accept all these things as historical accounts?"[4] Such a view is the result of the higher critical approach. This approach analyzes the language and text of the Bible as if it were an ordinary book, using the presuppositions of correlation, analogy, and criticism with their resultant methods of source, form, redaction, and tradition criticism and the like, in order to determine what actually happened.

At this point, it is helpful to review what is meant by the term *history.* It is a single word in English, but German scholarship has developed it along two distinct lines: *Historie* and *Geschichte. Historie* determines the facts of events and how they actually took place in the past. *Geschichte* is the way in which historians determine what those events mean.[5]

If in the historical investigation of a text, the supernatural was part of the event that took place, it ought not to be accepted as *Historie* or fact but might still be considered *Geschichte* in the sense of how the later writers of the Bible interpreted the past. For example, the Israelites' crossing of the Red Sea is described as an event in which God intervened by parting the Red Sea. Critics "tend to emphasize the natural rather than the supernatural aspects of the phenomenon."[6]

This emphasis on the natural undermines the event itself. To overcome the difficulty this causes to the believer, theologians introduced a third dimension called *Heilsgeschichte,* or salvation history. It takes the metanarrative, from Creation to consummation, as salvation history, decoupling it from the *Historie*'s facts and events. In this way, Gerhard von Rad differentiated between the historical kernel of history (*Historie*) and the kerygmatic picture of Israel's history as perceived by the biblical writers through the work of Yahweh. For Rad, "There are no *bruta facta* at all; we have history only in the form of interpretation, only in reflection."[7] Of supreme importance to this line of thinking is the theology *behind* the event, not the event itself. Whether or not an event occurred is incidental to the message.

The separation between *Historie* and salvation history introduces a dichotomy between actual historical events and theology, between what actually took place in history and matters of faith. It also raises several questions. Are biblical faith and history separable? Are theology and history separable? These questions led to the crux of the issue. Does it matter whether the events in the Bible took place? Some theologians answer with a resounding, "Yes, it does matter what took place!"

In a critique of von Rad's double tracking of secular history and kerygmatic history that is theologically meaningful, Franz Hesse insisted that faith must rest upon "that which has actually happened and not that which is confessed to have happened but about which we have to admit that it did not happen in that way."[8] To be sure, Hesse was not abandoning the historical-critical method, just insisting that only that which can be determined to have actually happened matters theologically.[9]

The historical-critical method, in its attempt to distinguish *Historie* from salvation history, precipitated a crisis in theology. One response to the European hypercriticism of the Old Testament was the work of Albright, Wright, and Bright, who insisted that "in biblical faith, everything depends on whether the central events actually occurred."[10] However, the movement failed to extricate itself from historical criticism. The Darwinian model of origins was adopted, essentially denying the foundational view of Creation.

Consequently, the dichotomy between history and divine intervention was never overcome. History could not be the authenticating factor of revelation but biblical revelation is self-authenticating. Scripture itself should be used to interpret Scripture and must remain captive to its internal basis for understanding. This internal appeal does not deny the importance of history but elevates the God who indeed intervenes in the historical nexus of time and space.[11]

The Protestant view is that God's acts are intrinsic in His spoken Word. The two cannot be separated. If Scripture is not trustworthy on historical statements, how can it be trusted on theological and spiritual questions? Two brief examples highlight the crucial relationship between history and theology.

The historical David and theology

In 1992, Philip R. Davies of the University of Sheffield declared that "the biblical 'empire' of David and Solomon has not the faintest echo in the archaeological record—as yet"[12] and claimed David and Solomon were mythical figures. The next year, in 1993, excavators in Israel's northern border city of Tel Dan found part of a large basalt stela inscribed by a king of Aram (Syria), recording a victorious battle against the territories of Israel and Judah.[13] Two more fragments were discovered the following year. The main inscription found, which had been reused in a later wall outside the city gate, dated to the late ninth century B.C. during the divided monarchy.[14] The Dan stela records this victory against the "king of Israel" and against the "house of David." The phrase "house of David" was subsequently identified in 1994 by André Lemaire in line 31 on the Moabite Stone found in Dhiban, Jordan.[15] Later, Anson Rainey identified the name *David* in line 12 of the same text.[16] The "house of David" is the phrase that the Bible consistently uses to refer to the southern kingdom of Judah (2 Samuel 2:11; 5:5; 1 Kings 12:20–26; 2 Chronicles 8:11). More significantly, in both of these inscriptions, the phrase "house of David" identifies the founder of the Judean line of kings more than a century after David's existence. Finally, K. A. Kitchen suggests that "the heights of David" is a toponym listed among the Negev sites mentioned in the Shishak reliefs at the Temple of Amun at Karnak in Egypt.[17] It is remarkable that in a matter of a few years, not one but four separate references to David were identified by scholars in Egyptian, Aramean, and Moabite inscriptions, testifying to the foundational influence of this early Israelite king.

Today, few scholars argue that David did not exist. But what if he was a fictional character? What if his kingdom was less than the Bible describes? Here are a few points to consider in response to these questions. Without David, who would defeat the Philistines, bringing them under control after decades of antagonism and conflict (1 Samuel 17; 23; 2 Samuel 5; 1 Chronicles 18:1)?[18] Without David, there would be no conquest of the Jebusite city of Jerusalem and its establishment as the capital that still survives three thousand years later (2 Samuel 5). Without David, seventy-eight psalms would be missing from the liturgy of Israelite worship, impoverishing synagogues and churches around the globe. Finally, what about the promised Messiah who was to come through the line of Jesse and David (Isaiah 11:1–10; Revelation 22:16)?[19] No other person is mentioned more frequently throughout the Old and New Testaments than David, from the earliest references in Ruth to the final chapter of Revelation.[20] His son Solomon built the temple in Jerusalem; refortified the cities of Megiddo, Hazor, Gezer, and Jerusalem (1 Kings 9:15); and established an extensive trade network, exponentially increasing the wealth of Israel. Without David, the Bible would have to be completely rewritten.[21]

The Cross, the Resurrection, and theology

History in and of itself is not revelatory; it needs to be revealed and explained. This is not a subjective enterprise; it requires divine revelation to interpret history. The cross does not, in and of itself, tell us anything about the meaning of the historical event. During the Roman era, thousands of people died futile deaths on crosses. After the revolt by Spartacus, the Romans, under Crassus, lined the Appian Way from Rome to Capua with six thousand crucified individuals.[22] So what was one more crucifixion in Jerusalem? And what separated Jesus of Nazareth from the other two thieves who were crucified with Him? It is only through the revelation of the Bible that the meaning of the cross becomes certain, and that certainty is based on the historical reality of the Old Testament prophecies and their fulfillment in Jesus Christ. That is why the New Testament writers emphasize not only the reality of the cross and the resurrection but also its connection to the typology of the lamb, sacrificed for generations by faithful Israelites and fulfilled on Passover Friday, A.D. 31.

The Gospels painstakingly connect the historical events of Christ's life with the statements made concerning Him in the law and the prophets. The Gospels offer history, prophecy, and personal witnesses as validation of the events. They recount the Magi's study that led them to follow the star prophesied by Balaam (Numbers 24:17; Matthew 2:1, 2). They record Jesus' statements from the cross, echoing the Messianic prophecies that testify of the manner of His death (Psalms 22:1; 31:5). They relay the testimony of Mary Magdalene, who came to the tomb on Sunday morning and saw her risen Savior (Mark 16:9–11; John 20:11–18). They tell about the disciples' experience with Jesus on the road to Emmaus and how He expounded the Scriptures to them (Luke 24:13–27). They tell of His appearance in the upper room, eating together, and His exchange with doubting Thomas (John 20:24–29). Hundreds of eyewitnesses saw Jesus after His resurrection, and John says, "This is the disciple who testifies of these things, and wrote these things; and we know that his testimony is true" (John 21:24).

Addressing the Corinthian church, Paul reaffirms recent historical events:

> For I delivered to you first of all that which I also received: that Christ died for our sins according to the Scriptures, and that He was buried, and that He rose again the third day according to the Scriptures, and that He was seen by Cephas, then by the twelve. After that He was seen by over five hundred brethren at once, of whom the greater part remain to the present, but some have fallen asleep. After that He was seen by James, then by all the apostles. Then last of all He was seen by me also, as by one born out of due time (1 Corinthians 15:3–8).

He emphasizes the Gospel writers' testimony, providing scriptural evidence for Christ's death and the certainty of His bodily resurrection: "Now if Christ is preached that He has been raised from the dead, how do some among you say that there is no resurrection of the dead? But if there is no resurrection of the dead, then Christ is not risen. And if Christ is not risen, then our preaching is empty and your faith is also empty" (verses 12–14). For Paul, the reality of the Resurrection was the basis of the faith of Christianity. History, theology, and faith were inextricably linked. The connection to history and prophecy made the claims of the Messiah true.

History, meaning, and identity

The power of the study of history is that it seeks truth. It aims to discover what took place in order to determine its purpose and meaning. If God is reduced to timelessness and removed from space and place as an abstract idea or philosophy, then He cannot act in history, rendering it and our existence meaningless. The Greco-Roman culture, after millennia of pagan superstition and mythical thinking, was bankrupt for these reasons and resorted to the escapism of the circus and the Colosseum. Today, history is repeating itself.

How does this play out in real life? A movie based on a fictional story taking place on planet Earth, with spaceships and invading creatures from another planet (think *Star Wars* or *The Avengers*)[23] will not have the same impact as watching on live television the second plane crashing into the Twin Towers on September 11, 2001. In the same way, the power of the Bible is the reality of its witness. It is not a fictional story. God contends "that this was the only place he acted that had significance for human beings, that those actions were according to a consistent, long-term purpose [of love], that he was using the details of human-historical behavior to reveal that purpose, and that he was just as capable of using enemies as he was friends to accomplish his good purposes."[24] This interlinking of history and divine prophecy is found nowhere else in the world, ancient or modern. And it is this combination that makes the Bible unique.

1. By comparison, the number of places mentioned in the entire Koran is the same number already accounted for by Genesis 10 in the Bible.

2. For a comparison between biblical and mythical thinking, see John N. Oswalt, *The Bible Among the Myths: Unique Revelation or Just Ancient Literature?* (Grand Rapids, MI: Zondervan, 2009).

3. Gerhard F. Hasel, "The Problem of History in Old Testament Theology," *Andrews University Seminary Studies* 8, no. 1 (1970): 32–35, 41–46; Gerhard F. Hasel, *Old Testament Theology: Basic Issues in the Current Debate*, 4th ed. (Grand Rapids, MI: Eerdmans, 1991), 115–138.

4. Walter Dietrich, *The Early Monarchy in Israel: The Tenth Century B.C.E.*, trans. Joachim Vette (Atlanta: Society of Biblical Literature, 2007), 102, 103.

5. See J. Alberto Soggin, "Alttestamentliche Glaubenszeugnisse und geschichtliche Wirklichkeit," *Theologische Zeitschrift* 17 (1961): 385–398; J. Alberto Soggin, "Geschichte, Historie und Heilsgeschichte im Alten Testament," *Theologische Literaturzeitung* 89 (1964): 721–736.

6. J. Maxwell Miller, *The Old Testament and the Historian* (Philadelphia: Fortress Press, 1976), 17.

7. Gerhard von Rad, "Antwort auf Conzelmanns Fragen," *Evangelische Theologie* 24, no. 7 (1964): 393; cf. Gerhard von Rad, *Old Testament Theology*, vol. 1 (New York: Harper and Row, 1962), 106–111.

8. Franz Hesse, "Kerygma oder geschichtliche Wirklichkeit?" *Zeitschrift für Theologie und Kirche* 57, no. 1 (1960): 26.

9. In maintaining the historical-critical method as the means to determine what was historical, Hesse "apparently does not recognize that the historical-critical version of Israel's history is also already interpreted on the basis of historico-philosophical premises." Hasel, *Old Testament Theology*, 119. In other words, he, too, is bound by the presuppositions of the historical-critical method that ultimately denies God's divine intervention in human history.

10. G. Ernest Wright, *God Who Acts: Biblical Theology as Recital*, Studies in Biblical Theology 8 (London: SCM, 1952), 126, 127; cf. G. Ernest Wright, *The Old Testament Against Its Environment*, Studies in Biblical Theology 2 (London: SCM, 1950); G. Ernest Wright and Reginald H. Fuller, *The Book of the Acts of God: Contemporary Scholarship Interprets the Bible* (New York: Doubleday, 1957).

11. Gerhard F. Hasel, "Biblical Theology Movement," in *Evangelical Dictionary of Theology*, ed. Walter A. Elwell (Grand Rapids, MI: Baker, 1984), 149–152; cf. Brevard S. Childs, *Biblical Theology in Crisis* (Philadelphia: Westminster Press, 1970).

12. Philip R. Davies, *In Search of "Ancient Israel"* (London: Continuum, 2006), 54.

13. Avraham Biran and Joseph Naveh, "An Aramaic Stele From Tel Dan," *Israel Exploration Journal* 43, nos. 2, 3 (1993): 81–98; Avraham Biran and Joseph Naveh, "The Tel Dan Inscription: A New Fragment," *Israel Exploration Journal* 45, no. 1 (1995): 1–18.

14. Gary A. Rendsburg, "On the Writing ביתדוד [BYTDWD] in the Aramaic

Inscription From Tel Dan," *Israel Exploration Journal* 45, no. 1 (1995): 22–25.

15. André Lemaire, " 'House of David' Restored in Moabite Inscription," *Biblical Archaeology Review* 20, no. 3 (May/June 1994): 30–37.

16. Anson F. Rainey, "Mesha' and Syntax," in *The Land That I Will Show You: Essays on the History and Archaeology of the Ancient Near East in Honor of J. Maxwell Miller*, ed. J. Andrew Dearman and M. Patrick Graham (Sheffield: Sheffield Academic Press, 2001), 287–307.

17. K. A. Kitchen, "A Possible Mention of David in the Late Tenth Century B.C.E., and Deity *Dod as Dead as the Dodo?" *Journal for the Study of the Old Testament* 22, no. 76 (December 1997): 39–41.

18. On the extended life and final demise of the Philistines in the archaeological record, see Seymour Gitin, "Philistia in Transition: The Tenth Century BCE and Beyond," in *Mediterranean Peoples in Transition: Thirteenth to Early Tenth Centuries BCE*, ed. S. Gitin, A. Mazar, and E. Stern (Jerusalem: Israel Exploration Society, 1998), 162–183; Seymour Gitin, "Philistines in the Books of Kings," in *The Books of Kings: Sources, Composition, Historiography and Reception*, ed. André Lemaire and Baruch Halpern (Leiden: Brill, 2010), 308, 309.

19. On the Messianic descriptions pertaining to David, see Philip E. Satterthwaite, "David in the Books of Samuel: A Messianic Hope," in *The Lord's Anointed: Interpretation of Old Testament Messianic Texts*, ed. P. E. Satterthwaite, R. S. Hess, and G. J. Wenham (Grand Rapids, MI: Baker, 1995), 41–65; Daniel I. Block, "Bringing Back David: Ezekiel's Messianic Hope," in Satterthwaite, Hess, and Wenham, *The Lord's Anointed*, 167–188; Daniel I. Block, "My Servant David: Ancient Israel's Vision of the Messiah," in *Israel's Messiah in the Bible and the Dead Sea Scrolls*, ed. Richard S. Hess and M. Daniel Carroll (Grand Rapids, MI: Baker, 2003), 17–56.

20. The name David is mentioned 1,087 times: 976 times in the Old Testament and 111 times in the New Testament.

21. For further study on the importance of David for the early history of Judah, see Yosef Garfinkel, Saar Ganor, and Michael G. Hasel, *In the Footsteps of King David: Revelations From an Ancient Biblical City* (New York: Thames and Hudson, 2018).

22. Appian, *Civil Wars* 1.120.

23. The idea of an impersonal "force" that is found throughout the universe is not a progression but is a regression to the paganism of the ancient mythic world of Egypt that sought to counterfeit the personal design of an all-loving God who intercedes for His people (e.g., the Exodus).

24. Oswalt, *The Bible Among the Myths*, 142.

The Bible and Prophecy

The Bible moves forward with a firm destination in mind. In its pages, the God of history is actively engaged with the nations and His people. He is also transcendent, able to see into future events, providing predictive prophecy to remind His people of their destination. The Bible is unique in that nearly 30 percent of its content is prophecy.[1] No other sacred text of any other world religion contains prophecy, because the worldview of these other religions is not one of a God who is transcendent and separate from creation but rather one of gods that are part of nature and have therefore always been part of creation.[2] Predictive prophecy provides the Bible with an internal mechanism to test the accuracy of the Bible's testimony. Prophecy assumes that

1. God is able to communicate future events that cannot be known to or predicted by human beings;
2. His knowledge is perfect concerning the events that will take place in the future; and
3. God has an ultimate plan for His people. Amos 3:7 states, "Surely the Lord God does nothing, unless He reveals His secret to His servants the prophets."

Classical and apocalyptic prophecy

There are two types of prophecy in the Bible. Classical prophecy was delivered by the prophets as a warning or to predict what would take place in the Old and New Testament times. The fulfillment of these prophecies was often tied to the response of the people. For example, the prophet Isaiah was sent to warn the northern kingdom of Israel that if the people did not repent and return to the Lord (1) "the riches of Damascus and the spoil of Samaria will be taken away before the king of Assyria" (Isaiah 8:4); (2) the cities would be "laid waste and without inhabitant" (Isaiah 6:11); and (3) God would remove "men far away, and the forsaken places" would be "many in the midst of the land" (verse 12). The prophets Amos and Hosea brought pointed rebukes and calls to repentance, warning that "Israel shall surely be led away captive from their own land. . . . Thus says the LORD: . . . 'Israel shall surely be led away captive' " (Amos 7:11, 17).[3] The fulfillment of this prophecy was witnessed in the prophets' own lifetimes when Tiglath-Pileser III in 732 B.C. and Shalmaneser V in 722 B.C. invaded the northern kingdom and destroyed the capital of Samaria and many other cities. We can still see the results of those destructions when excavating ancient cities such as Hazor, which ceased to exist and was subsequently not inhabited, just as the prophets predicted (2 Kings 15:29).[4] The people's lack of repentance allowed that judgment to occur.

A different outcome took place when Jonah went to Nineveh. The Ninevites did repent, and the Lord spared the Assyrian city and its inhabitants, both the people and the cattle of the field (Jonah 4:10, 11).[5] These prophecies were often specific in terms of outcome, yet they were conditional prophecies—dependent on the response of the people.

Apocalyptic prophecy, on the other hand, presents God's cosmic timetable for the fulfillment of His promise of the coming kingdom of God. It is not dependent on the actions of humanity and will take place exactly when and where God has ordained. The sixty-five specific Messianic prophecies were fulfilled in the life, ministry, death, and resurrection of Jesus

Christ "when the fullness of the time had come" (Galatians 4:4), just as outlined in Daniel 9:24–27.[6] The Messiah came even though Israel was not ready to receive Him. "The time prophecies in Daniel and Revelation which point towards the time of the end and the Second Coming are independent of any human response. In apocalyptic prophecy we become 'spectators to events on a world stage; we are seeing the divine foreknowledge unfold the course of the future.' "[7]

Apocalyptic prophecy is also characterized by long-range prophecies that have only a single fulfillment in history and cannot have multiple fulfillments. For instance, the seventy-week prophecy of Daniel 9 only had one fulfillment in Jesus Christ. Likewise, the 2,300 "evenings and mornings" of Daniel 8:26 and "a time and times and half a time" of Daniel 7:25 also have a single fulfillment that culminates in Jesus Christ entering the Most Holy Place of the sanctuary on October 22, 1844. This only occurs once in cosmic history.

Another aspect of apocalyptic prophecy is typology. Typology focuses on actual persons, events, or institutions of the Old Testament that are founded in a historical reality and point forward to a greater reality in the future. The use of typology as a method of interpretation goes back to Jesus and the New Testament writers. They understood that "the meaning of single events can often be fully understood only in the light of their consequences in later history" and that "typology and prophecy are twin sisters, both pointing forward."[8] The safest guide to recognizing a type and antitype is when an inspired Bible writer identifies them. Otherwise, subjectivity and human imagination can venture beyond God's intent.

For example, in Hebrews 9:11–15, Jesus is referred to as the High Priest, "the Mediator of the new covenant" (verse 15) who "entered the Most Holy Place once for all, having obtained eternal redemption" (verse 12). The type of the Old Testament sanctuary and its annual Day of Atonement service was fulfilled by the antitype of Jesus Christ, the perfect High Priest and the Lamb of God slain before the foundation of the world. It is to this event that all the sanctuary services pointed.

The final aspect of the sacrifice, death, and resurrection of Jesus culminated in 1844 when He entered the Most Holy Place of the true heavenly sanctuary. The use of typology in Scripture helped early Adventists reassess their assumptions about the nature of the sanctuary, and they discovered that it was not the earthly but the heavenly sanctuary, after which the earth's was patterned (Exodus 25:8, 9).[9]

Historicism and the year-day principle

The Protestant Reformation and the Seventh-day Adventist Church were both formed out of a renewed study of apocalyptic prophecy from a historicist perspective of interpretation.[10] Historicism is the oldest known method of prophetic study, originating from the text of Scripture itself and the biblical writers. It is described as "the continuous historical method of prophetic interpretation because it understands biblical prophecy to be continuous and consecutive as regards the predicted sequences of empires and events in the books of Daniel and Revelation."[11] Prophecy moves forward from the time of the biblical writer until the time of the end, and it does so without breaks or gaps in the process. Historicism has been the time-honored method of prophetic interpretation until the twentieth century.[12] In this chapter, we will look at how the historicist interpretation relates to the identification of the Seventh-day Adventist Church as the remnant church of Bible prophecy.

A key element of the historicist position is the year-day principle as applied to prophetic interpretation.[13] This principle has been applied to the time prophecies of Daniel and Revelation by many scholars over the centuries.[14] They derived the principle from several key texts and from the immediate context of the prophecies themselves.

The immediate context of Daniel's prophecies indicates that they point toward the "time of the end" (Daniel 8:17, 19, 26; 11:35; 12:1, 9). This means that the time indicators need to be interpreted accordingly. In addition to the immediate context of Daniel, two key texts provide the basis for the year-day principle. Numbers 14:34 contains a judgment by God that for every day that Israel spied out the land of Canaan (forty days), they would need to spend one year bearing the guilt of rejecting God's promise that they would conquer the land. As a result, the first generation of Israelites would spend forty years bearing their guilt. This case of classical prophecy moves from a past day to a future year; in apocalyptic prophecy, a future day stands for a future year. Ezekiel 4:6 contains God's instructions to the prophet Ezekiel: he should bear the iniquity of the house of Judah for forty days, "a day for each year." Strengthening the year-day principle are a number of linguistic connections between Numbers and Ezekiel:

1. In both, the act of "bearing" and the "evil" borne are written similarly.
2. Both passages are introduced with a phrase referring to "the number of the days."
3. In both, the concept of "each day for a year" is expressed with the reduplicated phrase "day for the year, day for the year."[15]

Numbers and Ezekiel are not apocalyptic books, so the year-day principle is clearly spelled out.

In contrast, in Daniel and Revelation

> the expressions "time, times, and half a time" (Dan 7:25; 12:7; Rev 12:14), "forty-two months" (Rev 11:2; 13:5), and "one thousand two hundred and sixty days" (Rev 11:3; 12:6) all apply to the same time period. . . .
>
> The only commonly used measure of time not used in the prophecies of Daniel and Revelation is the year. Days, weeks, and months, are referred to, but not the time unit "year." The most obvious explanation is that the "year" is the unit symbolized throughout these prophecies.[16]

Three other elements support the year-day principle in

Daniel and Revelation: the use of symbols, long time periods, and peculiar expressions. The symbolic nature of the beasts and horns representing kingdoms suggest that the time expressions should also be understood as symbolic. The fact that the kingdoms described spanned several centuries indicates that these were not to be interpreted as literal days, months, or times/years but as longer periods of time. Finally, the peculiar expressions used to designate these periods suggest a nonliteral, symbolic interpretation. It is no coincidence that all three expressions, once the year-day principle is applied, add up to exactly 1,260 years, confirming the prophetic interpretation of this period. If, on the other hand, the figures are taken literally as three and a half years or six and a half years, there would be no historical context where these periods would fit. Nor are they "capable of reaching anywhere near this final end time. Therefore, these prophetic time periods should be seen as symbolic and standing for considerably longer periods of actual historical time extending to the end time."[17]

Most commentators on the book of Daniel agree that the seventy-week prophecy of Daniel 9:24–27 could not have been fulfilled in a literal seventy weeks (one year and five months). This must be a longer period of historical time. Applying the year-day principle, this corresponds perfectly to the prophetic ministry, death, and final rejection of Jesus. "The command to restore and build Jerusalem" took place in 457 B.C. at the command of Artaxerxes (verse 25).[18] The time frame of the phrase "until Messiah the Prince, there shall be seven weeks and sixty-two weeks" (verse 25) pinpoints the beginning of Christ's ministry in A.D. 27, exactly 483 years after Artaxerxes's decree. "And after the sixty-two weeks Messiah shall be cut off, but not for Himself" (verse 26) is a prophecy that is fulfilled in the event of the Crucifixion, which occurred in the middle of the seventieth week, precisely in A.D. 31.[19] The end of that seventieth week came when the judgment of the rejection of the Messiah was pronounced by Stephen, who was stoned at the command of the Sanhedrin (Acts 7:59). The prophecy of Daniel 9:24–27 demonstrates the validity of the year-day principle.[20]

It should also be pointed out that by the second century B.C., the year-day principle was already actively in use by early Jewish interpreters, as referenced in Jewish Hellenistic literature, manuscripts found among the Dead Sea Scrolls in Qumran, and Josephus, among others.[21] This indicates that this crucial element of the historicist interpretation of prophecy was understood before the time of Christ.

The 1,260- and 2,300-day prophecies

Revelation 12 provides a concise overview of the 1,260 years of persecution against the woman (the church) by the dragon (Satan), resulting in his attempt to wipe out "the rest of her offspring," the remnant church (verse 17). The timing of the movement was inextricably tied to prophecy occurring *after* the 1,260 days/years of papal supremacy (A.D. 538–1798) and the rise of Protestant America. The two distinctive marks of the remnant are that they would "keep the commandments of God" and "have the testimony of Jesus" (verse 17).

The 2,300-day prophecy is crucial to our understanding of the sanctuary message. It also relies heavily on the year-day principle. According to Daniel 8:14, "For two thousand three hundred days; then the sanctuary shall be cleansed." The term *days* is literally "evenings-mornings." It has been aptly demonstrated that this is a twenty-four-hour day and does not refer to the morning and evening sacrifices at the temple (which preterists suggest took place during the reign of Antiochus Epiphanes IV).[22] In short, the *tāmīd*, or daily sacrifices, always occurred in the mornings and evenings, not the evenings and mornings. There is no support for the 2,300 evenings-mornings to be divided into two sacrifices, creating a new number of 1,150. In fact, the days of Creation, which represent twenty-four-hour periods of time, are designated consistently as "the evening and the morning" (Genesis 1:5, 8, 13, 19, 23, 31). Finally, Antiochus Epiphanes IV desecrated the temple for only three years, which makes only 1,080 days, not 1,150. The 2,300 days, understood in the context of the year-day principle, should be taken as whole time periods.[23]

How to Interpret Scripture

The identity of Seventh-day Adventism as a prophetic latter-day movement has its foundations in the historicist interpretation of the predictive prophecies of Daniel and Revelation. The bitter experience of the Great Disappointment led Millerite Adventists to a renewed study of the books of Daniel and Revelation in order to search for what they had missed when Jesus failed to return. Discovering that the Advent experience was predicted in Revelation 10:9, 10 was a great comfort to them. They could see that the devouring of Daniel's prophecies, finding them sweet as honey in the mouth but bitter in the stomach, was precisely their experience. William Miller had accurately made his calculations, but he had misapplied the event.

Nevertheless, Miller's hermeneutic for prophetic interpretation was strongly endorsed by Ellen G. White and our pioneers. He laid out several important principles for prophetic interpretation that were based on the *sola Scriptura* principle and the historicist interpretation of prophecy. Some of the principles Miller insisted on are the following:

1. Every word must have its proper bearing on the subject presented in the Bible (Matthew 5:18);
2. All Scripture is necessary, and may be understood by diligent application and study (2 Timothy 3:15–17);
3. Nothing revealed in Scripture can or will be hid from those who ask in faith, not wavering (Deuteronomy 29:29; Matthew 10:26, 27; 1 Corinthians 2:10; Philippians 3:15; Matthew 21:22; John 14:13, 14; 15:7; James 1:5, 6; 1 John 5:13–15);
4. To understand doctrine, bring all the scriptures together on the subject you wish to know, then let every word have its proper influence; and if you can form your theory without a contradiction, you cannot be in error (Isaiah 28:7–29; 35:8; Proverbs 19:27; Luke 24:27, 44, 45; Romans 16:26; James 5:19; 2 Peter 1:19, 20); and
5. Scripture must be its own expositor, since it is a rule

of itself (Psalms 19:7–11; 119:97–105; Matthew 23:8–10; 1 Corinthians 2:12–16; Ezekiel 34:18, 19; Luke 11:52; Malachi 2:7, 8).[24]

6. If you find every word of a prophecy (after the figures are understood) is literally fulfilled, then you may know that your history is the true event. But if one word lacks a fulfillment, then you must look for another event or wait for its future development. For God takes care that both history and prophecy agree so that the true, believing children of God may never be ashamed (Psalm 21:5; Isaiah 14:17–19; 1 Peter 2:6; Revelation 17:17; Acts 3:18).[25]

Careful Bible study resulted in the five distinct pillars of the Seventh-day Adventist Church: the Sabbath, the Second Coming, the sanctuary, the state of the dead, and the Spirit of Prophecy. The combination of these biblical doctrines with the three angels' messages are understood today to give the Seventh-day Adventist Church its message and mission.[26]

---

1. J. Barton Payne, *Encyclopedia of Biblical Prophecy* (Grand Rapids, MI: Baker, 1973), 674, 675, lists 1,239 prophecies in the Old Testament and 578 prophecies in the New Testament, for a total of 1,817. These encompass 8,352 verses or 26.83 percent of the Bible.

2. John N. Oswalt, *The Bible Among the Myths* (Grand Rapids, MI: Zondervan, 2009), 47–110.

3. Brevard S. Childs, *Isaiah and the Assyrian Crisis* (London: SCM, 1967).

4. Peter Dubovsky, "Tiglath-Pileser III's Campaigns in 734–732 B.C.: Historical Background of Isa 7; 2 Kgs 15–16 and 2 Chr 27–28," *Biblica* 87, no. 2 (2006): 153–170; for the annals, see Hayim Tadmor, *The Inscriptions of Tiglath-Pileser III, King of Assyria*, 2nd ed. (Jerusalem: Israel Academy of Sciences and Humanities, 1994); cf. Amnon Ben-Tor, "Excavating Hazor, Part One: Solomon's City Rises From the Ashes," *Biblical Archaeology Review* 25, no. 2 (March/April 1999): 37.

5. Gerhard F. Hasel, *Jonah: Messenger of the Eleventh Hour* (Mountain View, CA: Pacific Press®, 1976).

6. On the sixty-five Messianic prophecies, see Walter C. Kaiser Jr., *The Messiah in the Old Testament* (Grand Rapids, MI: Zondervan, 1995).

7. Gerhard Pfandl, "The Pre-Advent Judgment: Fact or Fiction? (Part 1)" *Ministry,* December 2003, 20, who quotes from William G. Johnsson, "Conditionality in Biblical Prophecy With Particular Reference to Apocalyptic," in *The Seventy Weeks, Leviticus, and the Nature of Prophecy,* ed. Frank B. Holbrook, Daniel and Revelation Committee 3 (Washington, DC: Biblical Research Institute, 1986), 278.

8. Hans K. LaRondelle, *The Israel of God in Prophecy: Principles of Prophetic Interpretation* (Berrien Springs, MI: Andrews University Press, 1983), 35, 54.

9. Ellen G. White, *Christ in His Sanctuary* (Nampa, ID: Pacific Press®, 2009).

10. See Leroy Froom, *The Prophetic Faith of Our Fathers*, vols. 1–4 (Washington, DC: Review and Herald®, 1950–1954).

11. Gerhard F. Hasel, "Israel in Bible Prophecy," *Journal of the Adventist Theological Society* 3, no. 1 (Spring 1992): 124.

12. On additional methods of interpretation, see Hasel, "Israel in Bible Prophecy," 121–130.

13. Gerhard Pfandl, "In Defense of the Year-Day Principle," *Journal of the Adventist Theological Society* 23, no. 1 (2012): 3–17.

14. Leroy Froom, *The Prophetic Faith of Our Fathers*, vol. 4 (Washington, DC: Review and Herald®, 1954), 784–851.

15. William H. Shea, *Selected Studies on Prophetic Interpretation*, rev. ed., ed. Frank B. Holbrook, Daniel and Revelation Committee 1 (Silver Spring, MD: Biblical Research Institute, 1992), 88.

16. Pfandl, "Year-Day Principle," 8.

17. Shea, *Selected Studies*, 73.

18. Siegfried H. Horn and Lynn H. Wood, *The Chronology of Ezra 7* (Washington, DC: Review and Herald®, 1953).

19. On the date of the Crucifixion, see Grace Amadon, "Ancient Jewish Calendation," *Journal of Biblical Literature* 61, no. 4 (December 1942): 227–280; Grace Amadon, "The Crucifixion Calendar," *Journal of Biblical Literature* 63, no. 2 (June 1944): 177–190.

20. Brempong Owusu-Antwi, *The Chronology of Daniel 9:24–27*, Adventist Theological Society Dissertation Series (Berrien Springs, MI: Adventist Theological Society, 1995).

21. Shea, *Selected Studies*, 105–110.

22. Siegfried J. Schwantes, " *'Ereb Bōqer* of Daniel 8:14 Re-examined," in *Symposium on Daniel*, ed. Frank B. Holbrook, Daniel and Revelation Committee 2 (Washington, DC: Biblical Research Institute, 1986), 462–474.

23. Gerhard F. Hasel, "The 'Little Horn,' the Heavenly Sanctuary, and the Time of the End: A Study of Daniel 8:9–14," in Holbrook, *Symposium on Daniel*, 430–433.

24. William Miller, *Miller's Works*, vol. 1, *Views of the Prophecies and Prophetic Chronology*, ed. Joshua V. Himes (Boston: Joshua V. Himes, 1841), 20, quoted in Ellen G. White, "Notes of Travel," *Review and Herald*, November 25, 1884, 738.

25. P. Gerard Damsteegt, *Foundations of the Seventh-day Adventist Message and Mission* (Grand Rapids, MI: Eerdmans, 1977), 299.

26. Damsteegt, *Foundations*.

CHAPTER

Dealing With Difficult Passages

Every Bible student has, at some point, encountered difficult Bible passages. This is unsurprising because anyone who
has interacted with another culture, worldview, or language
understands the challenges of communicating across these
boundaries. The same holds true for the content of the Bible. If
we understood everything in Scripture, we would be like God,
with no need for new insights. We would also lack the incen-
tive to grow in spiritual knowledge.

Compared to the Bible's eras, the time and places we live in
are vastly different. This fact poses challenges to interpreting
an ancient book rightly. While God has given enough evidence
to justify the trustworthiness and truthfulness of the Bible, no
amount of evidence will remove the possibility of doubt. If a
student wishes to indulge his misgivings, he will find many
opportunities to do so. A doubting spirit comes quite naturally
to human nature. In light of this tendency, it is worth noting
the importance of cultivating the proper attitude toward difficult passages of Scripture. Ellen G. White has described the
mind-set of people who trust their own opinions more than the
Word of God. She aptly writes:

When men, in their finite judgment, find it necessary

to go into an examination of scriptures to define that which is inspired and that which is not, they have stepped before Jesus to show Him a better way than He has led us.

I take the Bible just as it is, as the Inspired Word. I believe its utterances in an entire Bible. Men arise who think they find something to criticize in God's Word. They lay it bare before others as evidence of superior wisdom. These men are, many of them, smart men, learned men, they have eloquence and talent, the whole lifework [of whom] is to unsettle minds in regard to the inspiration of the Scriptures. They influence many to see as they do. And the same work is passed on from one to another, just as Satan designed it should be.[1]

The prophet then describes how this process of doubting subtly begins with a difficult passage of Scripture and quickly spreads to the rest of the Bible.

Beginning at Genesis, they give up that which they deem questionable, and their minds lead on, for Satan will lead to any length [that] they may follow in their criticism, and they see something to doubt in the whole Scriptures. Their faculties of criticism become sharpened by exercise, and they can rest on nothing with a certainty. You try to reason with these men, but your time is lost. They will exercise their power of ridicule even upon the Bible. They even become mockers, and they would be astonished if you put it to them in that light.

Brethren, cling to your Bible, as it reads, and stop your criticisms in regard to its validity, and obey the Word, and not one of you will be lost.[2]

Notice that in criticizing Scripture, our ability to criticize becomes sharpened until nothing is certain anymore. On the other hand, the energy invested in dealing with difficulties draws one deeper into the heart of Scripture. This deeper dive begins to reveal our willingness to embrace God's Word and obey its message.

Thus, difficult passages not only challenge us, but they also provide a unique opportunity to understand more thoroughly the biblical writers and God's message. Seen in this light, challenging and difficult passages in the Bible should make us grateful because they offer us a unique opportunity to grow in our understanding and lead us to implement in our lives what we have discovered. Many so-called mistakes in the Bible are not the result of God's revelation but are the result of our misinterpretations. Mistakes arise not so much from obscurity in the Bible but from the blindness and prejudice of the interpreter. History shows that problematic passages are not Christianity's most pressing problem. Instead, it is the failure of believers to accept the passages that are clearly understood.

Adventists do not try to prove that the Bible has no mistakes. One could prove that a newspaper article is free from all mistakes, but that would not demonstrate that the article is the Word of God. Bible-believing Christians hold the Bible to be the Word of God because Scripture affirms it, and Jesus and the apostles believed it. Ultimately, our conviction of its truth rests on the witness of the Holy Spirit, which confirms its truthfulness in our hearts and minds.

When difficulties are encountered, the Holy Spirit draws especially near. Space does not allow an examination of all the difficult passages, but their study is important, and the Spirit is ready to enlighten. (If you are interested in further research, several books and resources address the questions and issues raised by Scripture's difficult passages.[3]

How to deal with Bible difficulties

While we believe Scripture is trustworthy, we do not deny that some parts of Scripture are difficult to understand and pose a challenge to our mind-set and thinking. Even the apostle Peter acknowledged this fact when he spoke about Paul and his epistles: "Some things [are] hard to understand, which untaught and unstable people twist to their own destruction, as they do also the rest of the Scriptures" (2 Peter 3:16).

When it comes to difficulties and apparent mistakes in Scripture, we often see the Bible as the source of the problem. But we do well to note what the church father Augustine wisely stated: "If we are perplexed by an apparent contradiction in Scripture, it is not allowable to say, The author of this book [of the Bible] is mistaken; but either the manuscript is faulty, or the translation is wrong, or you have not understood."[4] We do not want to be like "untaught and unstable people," who twist Scripture to our destruction. Hence, we will look at a few important aspects that can help us as we encounter some difficult statements in Scripture.[5]

Do not assume there is no answer

It is important to remember that just because we do not have a solution to a particular problem that this does not mean there is no answer! Often, when we come across a difficult passage in Scripture, we might get the impression that we are the first ones to encounter the difficulty. But it is likely that other careful Bible students have studied the same Bible passage—perhaps even generations earlier, and even more thoroughly than we—and have noticed the same challenges. There is a good chance that others might have already found an answer, even though we might not be aware of it.

Furthermore, no serious person will claim to explain all Bible difficulties. It would be a mistake to conclude that what has not been explained yet can never be explained. For some questions, we do not have enough information available for a satisfactory answer. Some new archaeological evidence might shed light on some issues. Other problems might require more thorough research and inquiry of the biblical text and context. This task takes time and determination. Just because we cannot find an answer in five minutes, five days, or five months does not mean that there is no answer to that particular problem. The work and energy you invest in finding a solution to a vexing problem will probably do you more good than the solution itself.

In every case, approach difficulty with honesty and integrity, acknowledging that the problem you face does not have a satisfactory answer. Do not evade or ignore a problem, seek shortcuts to the answer, or twist the evidence. Patience is key. Sometimes we have to wait for an answer and trust God despite lingering questions. In this way, Bible difficulties can be an opportunity to develop a character in which God delights.

Do not confuse your fallible interpretation with God's infallible revelation

It is worth remembering that while the Bible is infallible, our interpretations are not. We can be mistaken in our interpretations and are prone to error. The meaning of the Bible does not change, but our understanding of it does. In light of this fact, we should be cautious about assuming that the currently dominant view of science is the final word on any given topic.

Evolutionary thought, for example, has become a widespread view in the scientific community. This has led to numerous difficulties with the biblical text. Is evolutionary theory really compatible with the biblical account of Creation and God's plan of salvation? Contradictions between popular views of science and the Bible are to be expected, especially if these scientific explanations completely rule out any divine agency. But this does not prove that there is a real contradiction between God's world and God's Written Word. While nature, according to the Bible, is God's creation and thus of divine origin, it is not inspired and continues to be affected by sin. Therefore, according to Ellen G. White, "the book of nature is a great lesson book," but it should be used "in connection with the Scriptures."[6] This means that God's special revelation in Scripture has precedence over natural revelation in creation. Scripture is superior to nature, for it is God's inspired witness. Hence Scripture, not evolutionary science, should be the normative source for understanding the origin of the world.[7] "When professedly scientific men treat upon these subjects from a merely human point of view, they will assuredly come to wrong conclusions. . . . The greatest minds, if not guided by the word of God in their research, become bewildered in their attempts to trace the relations of science and revelation."[8] Therefore, we should have a "settled belief in the divine authority of God's Holy Word. The Bible is not to be tested by men's ideas of science. Human knowledge is an unreliable guide. Skeptics who read the Bible for the sake of caviling, may, through an imperfect comprehension of either science or revelation, claim to find contradictions between them; but rightly understood, they are in perfect harmony."[9] Sometimes even long-held traditional interpretations of the Bible need to be restudied in light of what Scripture says on a given subject.

Interpret unclear passages in light of clear passages

In addition to having a teachable spirit, it is important to use sound hermeneutical principles in your study. First and foremost, always interpret unclear passages in the light of clear passages. Move from the clear to the less clear. Try to shed light from the clear passages of Scripture on those passages that are more difficult to understand. It is not advisable to build a doctrine on an obscure passage alone, and it is never acceptable to obscure clear passages by casting on them a dark cloud from a difficult passage. Instead, clear passages should illumine those that are less clear. The following example illustrates this point.

On the issue of speaking in tongues, several statements in Scripture clarify the New Testament gift of tongues. It was the supernatural ability to proclaim the gospel in another known human language (Mark 16:17; Acts 2:1–13; 10:46; 19:1–7).[10] But in 1 Corinthians 12–14, we find some statements about glossolalia that are not so easy to understand. Rather than obscuring the clear passages in Acts with the ones in 1 Corinthians 12–14, the clear and unambiguous passages should be allowed to shed light on the more difficult. Since the same words for "speaking in tongues" are used in Mark, Acts, and 1 Corinthians, and in light of other connections between prophecy and speaking in tongues in Ephesus and Corinth, the speaking in tongues in Corinth should also be understood as a supernatural gift of the Holy Spirit to speak in a known foreign language. Unfortunately, it was a gift that was misused by a few church members who sought only to edify themselves.

Consider the context of a passage

Perhaps the most common mistake of Bible critics is to use texts out of their context. A seminary professor once told our class that if we are confronted with a difficult passage for which we have no answer, there is one approach that is always correct: What does the context say? A text without a proper context quickly becomes a pretext for one's own ideas.

While historical context should be considered, the most important context of a passage is its immediate context. Carefully examine the section, then the chapter, and beyond that, the broader context of the book. Ultimately, the entire text of the Bible will become the context of the passage, shedding light on the difficult subject.

In the end, two simple guidelines will help the serious Bible student make sense of difficult passages: First, reason from the clear texts to the ones that are less clear. Second, allow context to inform your study and illuminate the Word. The Holy Spirit will bless such study with light and peace.

---

1. Ellen G. White, *Selected Messages*, book 1 (Washington, DC: Review and Herald®, 1958), 17.

2. White, *Selected Messages*, 1:18.

3. Cf. Gleason L. Archer Jr., *New International Encyclopedia of Bible Difficulties* (Grand Rapids, MI: Zondervan, 1982); William Arndt, *Bible Difficulties and Seeming Contradictions* (St. Louis, MO: Concordia, 1987); John W. Haley, *Alleged Discrepancies of the Bible* (Grand Rapids, MI: Baker Books, 1984); Norman Geisler and Thomas Howe, *When Critics Ask: A Popular Handbook on Bible Difficulties* (Wheaton, IL: Victor Books, 1992); Walter C. Kaiser Jr. et al., *Hard Sayings of the Bible* (Downers Grove, IL: InterVarsity, 1996); R. A. Torrey, *Difficulties and Alleged Errors and Contradictions in the Bible* (Chicago: Bible Institute Colportage Association, 1907); F. F. Bruce, *Hard Sayings of Jesus* (Downers Grove, IL: Inter-Varsity, 1983); and from an Adventist perspective, Gerhard Pfandl, ed., *Interpreting Scripture: Bible Questions and Answers*, Biblical Research Institute Studies 2 (Silver Spring, MD: Review and Herald®, 2010); Harald Weigt, *Verstehst du auch, was du liest? Schwierige Bibelstellen erklärt* (Lüneburg, Germany: Advent-Verlag, 2002); and the resources on the Biblical Research Institute website: https://www .adventistbiblicalresearch.org/materials.

4. Augustine of Hippo, "Reply to Faustus the Manichæan" 11.5, in *A Select Library of the Nicene and Post-Nicene Fathers of the Christian Church*, ed. Philip Schaff, vol. 4, *St. Augustin: The Writings Against the Manichæans, and Against the Donatists* (Buffalo, NY: Christian Literature, 1887), 180.

5. See also the additional aspects discussed in Frank M. Hasel and Michael G. Hasel, *Adult Sabbath School Bible Study Guide: How to Interpret Scripture*, 2nd Quarter 2020, lesson 12.

6. Ellen G. White, *Christ's Object Lessons* (Washington, DC: Review and Herald®, 1900), 24.

7. Ellen G. White was clear: "Apart from Bible history, geology can prove nothing. Those who reason so confidently upon its discoveries have no adequate conception of the size of men, animals, and trees before the Flood, or of the great changes which then took place. Relics found in the earth do give evidence of conditions differing in many respects from the present, but the time when these conditions existed can be learned only from the Inspired Record. In the history of the Flood, inspiration has explained that which geology alone could never fathom." *Patriarchs and Prophets* (Mountain View, CA: Pacific Press®, 1958), 112.

8. White, *Patriarchs and Prophets*, 113.

9. White, 114.

10. On this biblical evidence, see the thorough study by Gerhard F. Hasel, *Speaking in Tongues: Biblical Speaking in Tongues and Contemporary Glossolalia* (Berrien Springs, MI: Adventist Theological Society, 1991).

CHAPTER

Living by
the Word of God

Leading believers into an obedient relationship with God is the ultimate goal of Scripture. In studying the Bible, we seek to follow God's Word faithfully and joyfully. Such faithfulness goes far beyond mere intellectual knowledge and theoretical assent. God does not use coercion to win hearts. With a clear and reasonable voice, He speaks to us through Scripture, winning our allegiance with divine love. Attentiveness to the Word of God results in loving obedience and banishes the fear of difficult passages. Instead, we are eagerly motivated to understand the biblical message more fully and trust God to enlighten our hearts.

Faith is a necessary condition for properly understanding and responding to the Bible. The writer of the epistle to the Hebrews states that "by faith we understand that the worlds were framed by the word of God" and that "without faith it is impossible to please Him [that is, God], for he who comes to God must believe that He is, and that He is a rewarder of those who diligently seek Him" (Hebrews 11:3, 6). Such faith is the practice of actively listening to God and His Written Word. This listening exercise brings an obedient response to the Word of God. Of course, this obedience is often hard won because our humanity naturally hesitates to do God's bidding.

How to Interpret Scripture

Be doers of the Word of God

By nature, we are disinclined to listen to God's Word and even less inclined to follow His will. God knows this tendency in us and is always pursuing our hearts; He is wooing us to accept His love and, through the power of the Holy Spirit, practice His will in our lives. The apostle James admonishes us, "But be doers of the word, and not hearers only, deceiving yourselves. For if anyone is a hearer of the word and not a doer, he is like a man observing his natural face in a mirror; for he observes himself, goes away, and immediately forgets what kind of man he was. But he who looks into the perfect law of liberty and continues in it, and is not a forgetful hearer but a doer of the work, this one will be blessed in what he does" (James 1:22–25).

Søren Kierkegaard makes an interesting comment on this passage.[1] The one who hears the Word of God and does it is like a person who looks at himself in the mirror and remembers what he sees. What kind of looking at oneself in the mirror of God's Word, Kierkegaard asks, is required in order to receive a true blessing? He replies that the reader benefits from looking at the Word only if the reader moves beyond inspecting the mirror to seeing himself or herself. But rather than being willing to see ourselves in the revealing mirror of Scripture, sinful human beings are prone to start inspecting the mirror.[2] When we start criticizing the mirror, we lose sight of our condition, our sin, and our need for salvation. There is something in the biblical text that reflects a divine reality—a true understanding of who we are so that we can see our need for God. If we only interpret the mirror and do not comply with its command, we deprive the Bible of its authority through our interpretation, and we are not pleasing God nor are we acting according to His Word. What good is such an interpretation? It is often nothing more than a defense of ourselves against the Word of God. In order to avoid seeing themselves in Scripture as they really are, some readers prefer either to look at the mirror or to project their own, more flattering, images onto Scripture.[3]

The relationship between the Holy Spirit and the Bible

The Holy Spirit makes the Written Word of God come alive and elevates the Bible as the ultimate and final norm for everything we believe. A walk in the Spirit—if it is led by the Holy Spirit—will always result in the fulfillment of God's commandments. "God's commandments are the shoes in which our love for God walks and finds its faithful expression"[4] (cf. Romans 13:10). Thus, the ultimate goal of interpretation is to follow the Word of God in our lives.

Therefore, listening attentively to the Bible must precede our preaching and teaching. When we listen with a willing and obedient heart, God speaks. When we are willing to obey, God acts. It is not *thinking* about *living* well but actually living well that counts with God. Our interpretation should not aim to correct God's Word; it should allow God's Word to correct us. Listening to and obeying the Written Word lead to truth and freedom, bringing God's stabilizing grace to our daily lives.

Reflecting on God's Word

During His ministry, Jesus healed and preached every day. Solitary prayer and Scripture sparked the spiritual strength He needed for His efforts to reach lost people (Mark 1:35; 3:13). It seems that our modern lives have become even more hectic than life was during Jesus' time. In fact, our lives have become "crazy busy."[5] Our busyness seems to get the best of us. Smartphones have turned us into digital addicts who are easily distracted from real life. The more we become digitally distracted, the more we become spiritually displaced.[6] While being extraordinarily useful—even helping us study and memorize Scripture—smartphones are also powerful gadgets that can pirate our lives and diminish our spirituality. In our hectic and crazy lives, we have to deliberately plan for quiet times with God when we are uninterrupted and have undisturbed time to reflect on God's Word.[7] Such quiet time brings a strength and spiritual vitality that nothing else offers. Time with God's Word, unhurried and unforced, brings you face-to-face with Jesus, your Friend and Savior.

How to Interpret Scripture

Memorizing God's Word

Reading the Word daily is crucial to growing in Christ. An important element in receiving the Word is storing it all day long in your heart for ready access. Unlike our grandparents, we grew up in a generation where memorizing long poems, influential literary passages, or texts of hymns was out of vogue. In fact, for many of our generation, memorization was equivalent to thoughtlessness. It seemed stupid. The mere repetition of passages without thinking was unattractive. But memorizing Scripture does not have to be negative. On the contrary, it brings many blessings when done with thoughtful determination. Our lives head in a godly and good direction when our minds are fortified with God's Word.

Ancient followers of God's Word understood this well. The psalmist said, "Your word I have hidden in my heart, that I might not sin against You" (Psalm 119:11). The biblical writers knew that God's "word is a lamp to . . . [our] feet and a light to . . . [our] path" (verse 105). They were aware that "the entrance of Your words gives light; it gives understanding to the simple" (verse 130).

God's Written Word is premium spiritual food. The words of Scripture lead us closer to His will. At the same time, they offer an effective barrier against sin and dark thoughts that lead us away from God. When we deliberately memorize Scripture, God's Word goes beyond our consciousness to the heart of our being. Memorization anchors the Word in our minds so that we naturally, reflexively, begin to live "by every word that proceeds from the mouth of God" (Matthew 4:4).

Through mindful memorization, God's Word resides in our minds and impacts our social interactions, continually orienting our souls. God's words, if memorized effectively, can be applied to new situations, informing our decisions and empowering us to follow God's will. When faced with life-changing choices, the words of Scripture can emerge into conscious thought and direct our actions. This consciousness of God's will is what Jesus spoke of when He urged us to *abide* or *dwell* in Him: "If you abide in Me, and *My words abide in you*, you will ask what you desire, and it shall be done for you. By this My Father is glorified, that you bear much fruit; so you will be My disciples" (John 15:7, 8; emphasis added).

Scripture memorization and prayerful reflection serve to guide us through the life-changing process of internalizing truth. A God-given hunger for scriptural wisdom encourages us to put biblical truth into action. Anxieties can be conquered, and spiritual fitness can be enhanced, equipping us to meet future needs and opportunities. These are the tangible benefits of Scripture memorization, and the advantages go even deeper. Memorizing the Word of God helps to place greater value on heaven than on earth. It naturally causes us to examine the focus of our hearts, bringing us closer to the heart of God.

There is incomparable power in the Word of God. It is a power that can move us out of our spiritual complacency, bringing comfort in times of sorrow and guidance through the complex labyrinth of life. Scripture memorization sharpens our spiritual insight. We hear the preaching of the Word of God more clearly. It increases our knowledge and stimulates our interest in spiritual things. Additionally, it leads us to worship God more deliberately and thoughtfully. God is pleased if we worship Him according to the Scriptures. Occasionally, even our prayers can be offered in the words of Scripture, praying for others with the very words of the biblical writers.[8]

Many people have found that putting Scripture to music enhances memorization. A pleasant melody anchors God's Word securely in our minds. Singing brings joy, lifting our spirits and dispelling the darkness.

Memorization, reflection, and decisive action are integral aspects of living by God's Word. Hermeneutical tools and thorough study are meaningless if they do not lead the student to a practical faith. As a church, we are called to humbly follow the words of Scripture, corporately upholding the authority of the Bible and allowing it to inform and guide our ecclesiastical decisions.

May we be a people who are daily inspired and challenged by the living Word of God. May we seek to progressively embody the meaning and significance of the biblical text in our sphere of influence. Changed by His powerful Word, may we in turn become agents of change for the kingdom of God. Let us be not only hearers but doers of God's Word (James 1:22).

1. Søren Kierkegaard, *For Self-Examination: Recommended for the Times*, trans. Edna Hong and Howard Hong (Minneapolis: Augsburg, 1940).

2. Kierkegaard, *For Self-Examination*, 23.

3. Kevin J. Vanhoozer, *Is There a Meaning in This Text? The Bible, the Reader, and the Morality of Literary Knowledge* (Grand Rapids, MI: Zondervan, 1998), 15, 16.

4. Frank M. Hasel, "What Does It Mean to Be a Seventh-day Adventist? A Short Theological Reflection," *Adventist Review*, April 30, 2019, 49.

5. See Kevin DeYoung, *Crazy Busy: A (Mercifully) Short Book About a (Really) Big Problem* (Wheaton, IL: Crossway, 2013).

6. See an excellent and balanced discussion in Tony Reinke, *12 Ways Your Phone Is Changing You* (Wheaton, IL: Crossway, 2017).

7. A practical tool that can help you learn to do this is Frank M. Hasel, *Longing for God: A Prayer and Bible Journal* (Nampa, ID: Pacific Press®, 2017).

8. See Hasel, "Reasons to Pray for Others," in *Longing for God*, 149–152.